Chokecherry Places

ALSO BY MERRILL GILFILLAN

Truck (Poems)

9:15 (Poems)

To Creature (Poems)

Light Years: Selected Early Work (Poems)

River Through Rivertown (Poems)

Magpie Rising: Sketches from the Great Plains

Sworn Before Cranes

On Heart River (Poems)

Satin Street (Poems)

Burnt House to Paw Paw: Appalachian Notes

Chokecherry Places

Essays from the High Plains

~

MERRILL GILFILLAN

Johnson Books
BOULDER

Published in the United States by Johnson Books, a division of Johnson Publishing Company, 1880 South 57th Court, Boulder, Colorado 80301. E-mail: books@jpcolorado.com.

9 8 7 6 5 4 3 2 1

Brief portions of this book appeared in earlier forms in *Sports Illustrated* and *River Walk,* a collection of photographs by William Wylie. "Simple Song" was first published in the chapbook *Coppers and Blues,* Plum Pit Press, 1997.

Cover design: Debra Topping
Cover illustration: watercolor of the Cheyenne River in South Dakota by Robert Penn

Library of Congress Cataloging-in-Publication Data
Gilfillan, Merrill, 1945–
    Chokecherry places: essays from the High Plains / Merrill Gilfillan.
        p.   cm.
    Includes bibliographical references (p.   ).
    ISBN 1-55566-227-7 (alk. paper)
    1. Natural history—High Plains (U.S.)
QH104.5.H53G55   1998
508.78—dc21   98-29457
                                                                                      CIP

Printed in the United States by
Johnson Printing
1880 South 57th Court
Boulder, Colorado 80301

 Printed on recycled paper with soy ink

Contents

SIMPLE SONG

Sit in the chokecherry patches,
the wild plum groves,
the original grasses.

In under the sweet-tempered
grasses. Chokecherry stands.
The tough plum patches.

In or next the wild plum groves,
the longstanding grasses. Box elder,
hackberry. The chokecherry patches.

Locus Pocus
(Bighorns to the West)

THERE IS A PLACE in the middle of that particular someplace near Pine Tree Station, Wyoming, a place that gives onto both the first conifer-dark edges of the Black Hills to the distant east and the Bighorn Mountains long and low far to the west. It is an undistinguished spot save for this precarious generosity of vista. *Spot* is the fitting word for it. It resembles much of east-central Wyoming: It has a flock of sheep grazing desultorily nearby — dirty, tired-out ewes with snow-white long-tailed lambs who gambol and nose the new world of sagebrush and saltbush — and a broken down, never-painted shack across the highway.

It is a place, a place where I have stopped for lunch, and little but a place. A sun-hot, dry, yang place not to get caught out in. It is a place enticing by virtue of its simple, splayed one-and-only, its one-of-a-kind configuration where topography bares and heightens the severe contingency of its details: a shard of dull myopic mirror; an empty vodka bottle in the ditch; a lamb dead in a gully. It is a place irreducible in its elementary amino blend of sun and dirt and witness, its blend of happenstance and the rock-solid inevitable: a broiled shoe with a provocatively well-worn sole beside a sassy pink penstemon.

West of this place, about one-third of the way to the Bighorns, rise the Pumpkin Buttes. Seen through field glasses they appear harsh and aloof, parched, flat-topped, with a sprinkling of pines on the upper slopes. They stand far from most everything, lunar and austere. Their name seems too delicate, too soft; it derives from the Cheyennes' name for them, "Gourd Rattle Buttes": once a healing ceremony involving large Arikara-style gourd rattles took place in a Cheyenne camp near the buttes and was long remembered.

The Bighorns beyond are more complicated. Binoculars pick up a slightly hazy, heat-licked field of pine and nonpine, vague Cezanne-like color folds, shadow creases and dark canyon cuts, streaks and swirls of granite, snowfields. A diagonal slash of white rock—or is it smoke? From this summary distance the Bighorns stand clearly as a range, an entity unto itself whose details must be left to the imagination: a poet/hermit up there somewhere beneath a cool pine, gazing off this-away, lifting her telescope to sweep the Pumpkin Buttes, muttering, "Aloof, … austere."

One place leads directly to another, thank the dancing deities. There are familiar places; remembered places, burnished as driftwood; imagined places; glimpsed, passerine places rootless as petrels; places we can never find again. There are places like stone and places like oil. There are sacred places rising from the sea level, more one-and-only than all the others. There is the birthplace and the homeplace, certifiable by the olfactory, and the final restingplace, and all the in-betweens of dovetailed scenery and sweet locus pocus.

And they all lead directly to others, both in a literal sense and a speculative one: the pull and curiousness of the Place/Otherplace interaction, that continual fermenting, rests at the base of a primal fictive capacity deep as daydream. The lookaway speculation that watches a carful of people recede down a narrow road and then concocts a likely story about their destination and doings is an instinctive reflex to fill or appease the uneasy void of not being everywhere at once. It is a small, odd-colored lightbulb above the head. Farmlights by night, the old shoe, Tennessee license plates set it off. It is a childlike process of managing the Almost-visible and the Just-over-the-rise. In open country like central Wyoming, it is nearly constant for the so-inclined.

(And up there, over there in the Bighorns, up one of those hazy canyons, there is a cranny that once held the mortal remains of a Cheyenne man named High Backed Wolf. High Backed Wolf was reportedly killed at the

Platte River bridge fight in 1865, when a party of Cheyennes rode south to protest the increasing white traffic into their lands and struck at an army detachment protecting the bridge, near presentday Casper. Returning north toward the Tongue River country, the Cheyennes, it is told, buried their casualties among the eastern Bighorns, including the man called High Backed Wolf.

Some fifty years later, when the Bighorns were full of cattle and sheep and their herders, a rancher on his rounds one day discovered what he called "a mummy" in a shallow cave. He looked it over—it was a fairly complete corpus—and decided to take it home, and later to the small museum in a nearby town.

The group who examined the skeleton noted a distinctive hump in the upper spine. Someone among them had heard of a Cheyenne named High Backed Wolf—and the slow low buzz of rumor and fancy led them to conclude that the humpbacked "mummy" must be his.

Several years later, the founder of the Hastings Museum in Hastings, Nebraska, while traveling the west, came upon and acquired the mummy with the resonant name. This was in the late twenties or early thirties, and the remains have been in Hastings ever since. Since the Hands-off Native Burials offensive of the 1970s, the display of High Backed Wolf's skeleton has been sealed off from public view awaiting legislation and legal precedents. And one of these summers or falls there

4

will be a small cortege climbing into one of those Big-horn canyons carrying the bundle of a humpbacked man back to his proper pine-scented venue.

The whole story has such a schoolboy disingenuous-ness and circus-tent yokel earnestness about it that it has almost no outrage intact. It seems business as usual in these hot dry parts, a mere fleeting mosquito bite on the dignity of the man with the hump, and the eventual return of the cortege a natural, inevitable justice worthy of a short prayer and a long feast. They may be up there right now for all I know.)

So, here between the broiled Wyoming shoe and the spider-filled vodka bottle in the ditch is a place, a place as good as any to sit and ponder the Bighorns. It is a place that, like many others on the plains, takes its pri-mary colors from the horizon and its siren outrigger referents. Webster's Dictionary: Place: Middle English, from Middle French: open space; from Latin *platea*, broad street; from Greek *plateia*, from feminine of *platys*, broad, wide, flat. This spot qualifies along those lines.

But it is pointless, even dangerous, to get carried away with it all; we might walk obliviously into a giant many-armed prickly pear. Space, place, needs circum-scribing by something other than the tremulous visual.

Say, place, human place, defined by earshot, one mead-owlark call in all directions. The rest is vista.

And another, parallel etymology: Sanskrit *prthu* (broad), narrowing handsomely into Latin *planta*, sole of the foot—always a sensible standard.

Two Nights
at Smeeth Lake

THERE IS SOMETHING in the unison of ducks—wild, unbroken ducks—that is reassuring as a breeze in aspens. I have been watching a small raft of redheads ride the modest mid-May chop on Smeeth Lake and wondering at the staunchly jaunty unison of the score of identical creatures in the binocular field. Strikingly handsome against indigo water in early evening sun, cut of the one mold and riding the one medium, they call me back again and again. They are a canny familial aggregate, delicate, sharp of bright yellow eye, utterly humorless, ready at any instant to leap and disappear, unbroken.

The sensation is much the same amid the huge waterfowl flocks along the Platte River in March. The endless lifting and settling, circling and gathering, the countless squadrons of ducks and geese in their perfect concentration and unarguable mission among the high jet trails evoke a sense of system that is both seamlessly closed and comfortingly sane.

But a small flock at rest like the one at hand is more intimate. I am the only person at Smeeth Lake and this is my flock. There is an occasional pair of Ruddy ducks farther out, but the redheads are for the moment *the* ducks, not just one aspect of a great hubbub. So I watch them until my eyes tire, and come back to them five or ten minutes later.

They make me think of all the popular calendar illustrations and color prints of ducks in their various postures that have graced cabins and living rooms and taverns for several centuries: mallards jumping from a pond, Wood ducks with wings set dropping to a wooded swamp. People can be taken with ducks who are taken with no other birds, partly because of, no doubt, the birds' high waterfowl visibility, as well as their popularity as hunted prey, but also, perhaps, because of this far-ranging and dauntless unison—one never sees a score of Blackburnian warblers traveling in aggregate.

And the ducks have a feel to them different from the large flocks of phalaropes I saw earlier this afternoon on another Sandhill lake to the south, thousands of birds swirling and tacking in tight formation, flashing above the water in a brilliant mathematical frenzy. The redheads are not breathtaking in that virtuoso phalarope-whirl or sandpiper-flock fashion; they show a more earthly gravity and perfectly adjusted aplomb.

Smeeth Lake is a major oasis in the Nebraska Sandhills not only by virtue of her water—there are many other lakes in the region—but because of her plentiful trees: dense acres of planted pines and a good number of deciduous trees on three of her shores, comprising the greatest stand of arboreal cover for miles in all directions. As a consequence, bird life is varied and abundant. There is a lot going on around my tent and picnic table this spring evening. Marsh wrens and Yellow-headed blackbirds dominate with their rattles and croons, but there is Yellow warbler song in the cottonwood overhead and from nearby trees I hear two vireos, orioles, Crested and Least flycatchers, catbird, bluebird, and Brown thrasher. A yellowthroat sings from a bush near the cattails.

Like all oases, Smeeth Lake has the sensation of continual departure and arrival, the subtle expectancy of a caravanserai. Most any airborn creature passing through the region will likely drop in for water and shade and respite from the Great Plains winds—new and unpredictable visitors at the gates.

Such as these two willets suddenly coasting in high from the west, one crying its piercing *pil-wil-willet* call over and over as they circle the lake, climbing to fall again in a slow floating arc against the dimming peach-colored sky. Every eye locks on them for a brief moment; it is a brash and applaudable grand entrance.

~

The next morning as I finish my coffee and pack my daypack for a hike, there is something new on the scene. I notice a flock of fast-moving birds coursing down the shore toward my camp and put the binoculars on them. It is a dozen Black terns sweeping the edge of the lake, chippering and darting as they feed. So starkly and abruptly new in the neighborhood, so handsome and sure, they seem almost piratical at first glance.

I walk off through the knee-high grasses around the southwest quarter of the lake. Low-slung flocks of Clay-colored sparrows flush lazily from the ground and alight in the scattered pines. There are numbers of Cedar waxwings and Swainson's thrushes in the campground grove and a grosbeak sings. But the warblers that set down in this two-square-mile habitat are always the greatest surprise. I hear an ovenbird singing from the pine stand and spot a redstart farther along the shore. And then, the great gift of the day—a bright male Parula in a Russian olive, head-high just ten yards off. He might have just pulled in this daybreak.

I climb away from the lake and into the sand hills on the south side. On a high one I clear the ticks off my trousers and look over the slow sogging source of the lake, the head of Pine Creek. It is a broad, brushy green lowland that at once reminds me of the willow-alder riverheads in the Rockies, with their thin-air Lincoln sparrow music.

From this sand hill all of Smeeth Lake and its groves are easily visible amid the bounding grasslands. As a plains oasis it is almost on the large side. There are many more plaintive examples. There is a place on the Pawnee Grasslands in Colorado where I have slept a few nights that on first impression appears to be nothing but five impoverished trees—two cottonwoods and three willows—spaced along a fifty-yard stretch of a generally bone-dry streambed. But after an hour in the lawnchair there, this hapless high plains toss-of-the-ecodice spot proves to be an oasis indeed. Those five raw-boned trees are the only trees for a long way and they stand, apparently, in close enough proximity to qualify as a loose and linear "grove."

Both Bullock's and Orchard orioles live there. Eastern and Western kingbirds raise broods in the same tree. There are Lark sparrows back and forth and a three-quarter-grown shrike family spilling out of the nest in a squat old willow. The population density is obviously high.

But the touch that highlighted the oasis syndrome, the urgency of tight quarters amid vast space, was the Swainson's hawk nest in the largest cottonwood. I had no idea she was in there until the first occasion she left the nest. As soon as she stirred, two pairs of kingbirds were on her in high attack form, sputtering and screaming, the eastern's red crown ablaze. Two white Swainson's nestlings fumbled and groped uneasily in the wake. It is difficult to imagine tighter quarters than a hawk and a kingbird sharing the same tree. This hysterical alarm scenario was repeated at least hourly throughout the day as the hawk came and went with food for her young. This took place in early July; the kingbirds obviously had no inclination to grow accustomed to their fellow tenant. The hawk mother must have been worn to a frazzle. But there they were in Murphy's Pasture, gutting it out like a terrier and a tomcat on a liferaft, in the cottonwood of their value-added fancy.

~

The immense and carefully targeted black cloud with the ominous furry-cellulite underside reached the lake at 2:00 P.M. I was watching a group of Eared grebes halfway across the lake when the west wind hit and the lake water was instantly whitecapped. Within one minute it was a savage blow, all visibility zero from the car where I took refuge, and then a great racket of slashing hail. The car rocked in the wind and the hail blasted in nearly parallel to the ground. Water oozed in the westside windows. It was a din, frontal, violent and brainless enough to be frightening. I knew there were at least two small fishing boats that had been caught on the

Two Nights at Smeeth Lake

water, and I wondered for a second what the Parula was doing through all this. But in seven minutes it was over. The hail slackened and the wind fell, leaving a simple solid rain; then a quick clearing.

I found the grebes minutes later, unruffled, several hundred yards downwind from their previous position. The hail was piled in shoals and troughs. A yellow-head dropped down to peck luxuriously at it as if it were a long-awaited manna-caviar.

Soon the sun was out full and I got out to stretch, but moments later the wind was back, a new one, dry and formidable, right out of the north this time. It blew from 2:30 till 5:00, so that I sat most of the afternoon at the driver's wheel doing my rudimentary Lakota grammar exercises, then browsing contentedly in Father Buechel's *Lakota-English Dictionary* and keeping an eye on the lake.

—*Wicazo kin tuktel yanka he?* (Where is the pencil?)
—*Wicazo kin akanwowapi mahel yanke.* (… on the table.)

I find the word for hail is *wasú*. Rain is *magáju*. The Red-headed duck is *magásniyanla*. The teal are named, I see, for their prominent facial markings rather than their wing patches: the blue-wing "White beside the eye" duck and the green-wing "Green on the temples."

It is interesting to see what a non-binoculared people call their birds. Many Lakota avian names refer of course to the dominant color of the creature: the barn and tree swallows are distinguished by belly color. But often there is more, and the primal naming process shows more wit and inspiration. The bobolink is called "skunk bird" because of the white markings on a black back. The redstart's name derives from the word for "playing cards"—certainly because of its habit of spreading and fanning its colorful tail. According to Father Buechel, among the Lakota a person who talks loud and angrily is compared to the Yellow-headed blackbird. A long-beezered man is a "curlew" as a wide-mouthed man is a "whip-poor-will."

And occasionally this cosmopolitan bird-sense and ornithological capital blossoms into a wonderful poetic generalization: *zitka´to*, the bluebird, imbues the idiom *zitka´to s´e ahiyaye*—"to pass by all in blue."

~

The sunset was a chilly one, an intense wintry pastel: a low belt of deep orange with a faint pale-blue liner above, it hung motionless and steely for what seemed a very long time. And the night was cold, near freezing; a full moon kept the yellow-heads and kingbirds calling intermittently the whole night through just above the tent.

Two Nights at Smeeth Lake

The chill gets me up and out early. A gauzy mist lies on the lake, slowly dissipates with the rising sun. The day is clear and the wind is down for the moment. I decide to make a pot of oatmeal with raisins.

At the waterpump I hear the latest visitor to the oasis, a Blackpoll warbler singing in the pine stand, just up from Venezuela via the Yucatan. And there, with my first cup of coffee, the Black terns are back, hawking cheerily near shoreline—familiar now, a part of things, indispensable old friends.

I sit in the welcome sun and leaf through the Buechel dictionary, the Father's lifetime work. I note in passing an odd but no doubt invaluable verb that is worth pondering: *Našká:* "to untie with the feet." And somewhere between *kiši´ca* ("to kick a dog from the house") and *kizu´zeca* ("to turn into a snake") I find the perfect morning coffee verb here at the oasis: *kiyo´nakijin:* "to arrive, to arrive and take refuge in with the others."

A Little-Known
Renewal Rite from 1988

I KNEW THE SON from Denver, but didn't know the old man. When the boy heard I was going to K.C. for a few days he told me his father was looking for a ride to Colorado and asked if I would consider bringing the old man back with me. He thought we would hit it off fine. I called the man—his name was Cornell—as soon as I arrived in K.C. and we made plans for the trip. He asked me if I would mind taking him back along the Republican River route across northern Kansas. Old route 36 most of the way.

I picked him up at his house Monday after lunch. He was a stout Southern Ute man about sixty, quiet but friendly. He had lived in K.C. for twenty-two years, working at a refrigerator plant. Cornell stuffed a duffel-bag in the trunk and we drove west. After we passed Topeka we cut off the big highway and went north to a lesser route. It was a sunny All Souls' Day.

Cornell finally sketched out his plan for the river road. He needed flicker feathers to make a prayer fan. Yellow flicker tail feathers in particular. He had the fan handle beaded and his friends in western Colorado had sent him some red flicker tails. But for the yellow ones he would have to get them himself, just enough to fill out the red ones in a pretty fireburst of a fan. If I would help him, he could do it on this trip; he knew the yellow flickers were to be found along the Republican valley, all the way across into Colorado.

We looked at the map and decided we would stop in Concordia, Kansas, for the night. It was a town pretty much right on the river. We took a motel room and ate supper and drove out just at sunset to the Republican River bridge a mile or so north of town. There was a fishermen's parking area near the bridge. We walked into the big grove of cottonwoods along the south bank and Cornell looked around. At last he located a tall dead cottonwood tree in a little clearing and said that would be a good place.

We went to sleep early and got up before daybreak, had quick cups of coffee, and drove in the chilly dark back to the bridge. Cornell took a small .22 rifle from his duffel and we walked quietly into the woods just as the eastern horizon was lightening. We proceeded straight to the old cottonwood snag and took position behind a nearby tree.

The first sound to break the silence was crow-call from upriver. In a few moments three of them flew into the dead cottonwood, looking around at the morning and calling humpbacked to the new day. Then they departed, and within half a minute a flicker swirled into the upmost branches, just coloring with the first full sun. When it was settled on its limb, Cornell slowly raised his rifle, making soft, barely audible semi-whistling sounds with his lips, and shot the bird. It fell forty feet to the ground with a faint thump.

We waited again. Several minutes later two flickers, then another, flashed into the leafless treetop. Cornell shot another one, then said we had better go, and walked over to retrieve the birds. He held them breast up in one palm and looked at them carefully, said they were the most beautiful bird he knew about. "Better than a pheasant." Then we slipped out to the edge of the grove, checked up and down the highway for cars, and hurried off just as full Kansas-light was spreading.

Soon we left the river as it bore in from the north and we settled in for a steady morning across Highway 36. Cornell examined the two flicker tails, smoothing and delicing them as we drove. He said his father once told him that yellow flickers were females, red ones males.

He began to talk about the peyote church he belonged to, and about the world of feathers, the trade routes and various techniques of peyote fan makers across the west. He described a magpie trap a man had constructed in Wyoming, a large cage whose modus resembled a fish trap set on end: the magpies jumped down into the trap to get the vegetable scraps (meat would draw skunks and coyotes), then couldn't fit through the narrow roof hole with their wings spread for flight. The Arapaho man rigged it up each winter when the plumage was prime, plucked only the middle two tail feathers, and released the birds unharmed.

Cornell told of fifth generation Mexican traders walking the streets of Taos with long tooled satchels carrying sets of perfect scarlet and blue macaw feathers. He told me about peyotists in Oklahoma drifting concealed in rowboats through backwater swamps to stalk water turkeys sunning on stumps, described the birds' resplendent "corrugated" tail feathers. And Kiowa men going out after dark among the mesquite thickets with stepladder and flashlights in search of scissortail roosts. The birds would sit unflinchingly under the flashlight beam while a spry hunter climbed the ladder and grabbed one and plucked the longest tail feathers, then threw the outraged bird into the air and retreated from its angry attacks.

We crossed Sappa Creek and Beaver Creek and stopped for lunch in St. Francis, Kansas. As soon as we entered Colorado, Cornell began readying his gear. We dropped south from 36 a few miles to a state hunting area he knew of, a sizable reservoir with good wooded cover around the edges. It was the dammed-up South Republican fork. After 250 miles we were back on the same stream six hours later and the flickers were still of the yellow variety.

A Little-Known Renewal Rite

I sat in the car lolling and daydreaming like an autumn cabbie while Cornell crept off secretively into the cottonwoods. He came back forty-five minutes later with two more birds. That would be enough, he said. He was obviously happy: four tails would fill out his fan in great style. And all from the same river! That was better yet. He stowed his rifle back in the duffel and we went on toward Denver. Cornell napped a little, now that his work was done, and when we got nearer to the mountains he looked over the brilliant squash-golden tails again, turning them in the sunlight, before placing them carefully in a flattened cardboard tube from a toilet paper roll—he had found it in the wastebasket at the cafe—and putting it away in his shirt pocket.

He insisted on being dropped at the Denver bus station. He would call his son from there, but wanted to get back home and finish his fan. He would tie the new yellow feathers every-other-one, in with the red. I left him at the depot about 5:30. He hobbled off with his duffel, checking his left breast pocket with a tap-tap of the hand. Fort Hays. Salina. Junction City. The downstream route. The express would get him into K.C. just about dawn.

Blackfoot Country

EACH TIME I DRIVE through Blackfoot country, each time I acclimate again to the particular cadence of those rolling plains and their various upthrusts, I begin to think of a certain trencher of food described by James Willard Schultz in one of his books. There is broiled grouse and fried trout, and biscuits with stewed dried apples, and the mysterious *depouille*, a hand-thick layer of suety fat from next to the bison tenderloin that is likened by Schultz to a sweet, cakey bread. Sometimes there is a rack of pronghorn ribs staked by the fire; sometimes a bullberry stew. It is a variable spread, called forth by the landscape. It is all Blackfoot food, northern plains food, and sooner or later the landscape calls it forth.

When I say "Blackfoot country" I mean the land between Calgary, Alberta, and Great Falls, Montana, from the edge of the Rockies to somewhere out near the Judith range. As land, much of it is no longer Blackfoot land, of course, but as country it is still Blackfoot country, country held in that people's collective memory, and country holding remnants of that people's presence and mentality.

To drive through it and think of such things — thoughts of "These hills held in those eyes" — is neither wistful, in the end, nor romantic, if done right. It involves no dreamy childish mimickry or cruel nostalgia. It is the simple recognition of a noetic presence now for the most part displaced. But it can be slippery to explain.

Rilke termed the Art of Looking, the discipline of seeing, *Augenwerk*. Moving through a landscape one looks, barring stupefaction or blindness. Looks for what? Food? (Peanut butter and black beans in the backseat.) Water? (Water jugs aplenty.) Love? (That's it.) And strength and ballast, spiritual sustenance and ease-of-heart and wind-in-sail. It is a tropism of the inner life, a leaning toward a solid grounding and precedent.

I have turned more than once for footing and exemplar to Ezra Pound, his ambulations through the troubador country of southern France, his look-abouts and craggy mulling on a phenomenon seven centuries gone. Moving through that wine and olive country, looking for what? "The vanished voices of Provence." "Vestiges of troubador culture." But, more than that, to "recover" the singular referential, wind-on-the-face ground of troubador song; to set physical foot on that solid ground and revitalize both the impetus and the context, as in river, hill, and weather. To experience, through that devoted "inspective energy," the exultation imbued in that landscape and only in that landscape.

~

Yesterday, up north in the Siksika country on Bow River, I got out of the car to walk over to the monument honoring Crowfoot, a Siksika leader in the nineteenth century. A weary sign points the way: "Crowfoot's Last Tipi—¼ Mile." Below the monument, a handsome hook of the Bow runs in a wide, deeply wooded bottom at the brittle edge of the Blackfoot town of Cluny. At the base of the marker a fawn-size weathered-unto-velvet skeleton lies among buffalo grass.

The river bottoms are, with the exception of an occasional field of blue flax, the only things that break the Alberta wheat monoculture, monotone. The Bow, the Little Bow, the Belly. The Red Deer River. The Porcupine Hills. All names from James Willard Schultz. He first seeded the Blackfoot landscape in my consciousness. My recollection while driving south from Vulcan that the Bow River was originally the "Beau" and the Belly River originally the "Belle" probably came from him.

I first read *My Life as an Indian* about 1955 at age ten. I have read it six or eight times during the forty years since, I suppose, as well as many of his other writings about the upper Missouri Blackfoot country of the 1870s and '80s. It was a major fertilization. I still think of him every time I see the Sweetgrass Hills on the skyline, and the Judith Mountains, and each time I cross Milk River or walk by the old Bozeman train station where he sometimes alighted. And even though they now come off the page for me as fiction rather than absolute account, the best of his stories still hold a freshness and first-person power that is stirring as only a story reflecting a world-well-loved can be stirring; simple, alfresco, unapologetically elegiac as some of Turgenev's sketches. I turn to them sometimes to freshen my faith in elemental narrative.

Once I made a minor detour to stop in Boonville, New York, and see his boyhood home, and a few years ago I climbed the hills above Two Medicine Creek on the Montana Blackfoot reservation to the bluffs where he was buried beside his Piegan wife in 1947.

~

The Crowfoot monument is one sort of Blackfoot presence. But they left songs, of course, as did their neighboring tribes on the plains, and names on the land if you track them down, find them. Song/poems at least as pertinent as the troubador versions these fin-de-siècle days, companionate songs with the evocative high relief of operatic arias like "Connais-tu le pays?"

> Are you going to Ree River?
> Are you packing up
> For Ree River? Setting out,
>
> Heading for? Is he leaving
> For Ree River? How many days
> There? How many hills?
>
> Are you riding for Ree River
> To find a girl?
>   (Cheyenne)

> "Where is that girl who danced that night?"
> "Out picking rosebuds for soup."
>   (Blackfoot)

> "My son
> I am from the south
> Where plums stay
> On the trees
> All winter long."
>   (Pawnee)

"Knee-Prints on the Banks-of-the Water"
The stars flew around like birds.

(Pawnee)

I am looking for my robe—
The skies are painted across it.

(Pawnee)

And the mysteriously moving and expansive Gray Crane lyric from a Blackfoot tale (it has a lucent pathos that makes me want to live forever):

The gray crane sings
"I Wish to be on Level Ground."

~

This morning early I drove down from Ft. McLeod, Alberta. Wild roses were blooming along the highway, sweet clover was in the air. Flocks of gulls swept the newly cut hayfields, following the mowers. Then the Belly Buttes took over the vista and jogged the etymologies. The buttes are an extensive jagged escarpment, eight or ten miles long, of modest height, but possessing that attention-catching *visited* look that bestows, on landscape, voltage.

But it was the color—a washed-out, striated rosy pink-white—of the escarpment face that got me thinking. Somewhere in Schultz he mentions, rather in passing as I recall, that the Belly Buttes were thought by the Blackfoot people to resemble a buffalo carcass stretched out, skinned, and ready to butcher. And, I believe, named accordingly. A fuzzy etymology, especially in the hearsay of memory. But there are the shimmering periwinkle-colored flax fields along the road, and the skeleton-remnants of several generations of old sun dance lodges standing on the green slopes between the buttes and the river.

~

What lives in a landscape beyond the hand-to-mouth is an exultation, over and over, *with* that landscape, an exultation yielding, sooner or later in any population, Song. To locate and make contact with the *genius loci*—Cutbank Creek or Poitiers—and to connect for a moment with those predecessors on the plane of Place-Sprung-from-Time is a soaring, but a sensible soaring. Song both sung and received. Red Deer River or Angoulême.

~

When I got on down to Browning, Montana, on the Blackfoot reservation, I stopped to eat a sandwich and read the local paper, the *Glacier Reporter.* There, in the

Letters to the Editor, is a missive from one Gene DuBray, a subchief of the tribe, deploring the purchase and sale of Indian sacred objects by whites, and then, lo, a paragraph devoted to James Willard Schultz! From which I quote:

"My great-grandfather Eli Guardipee, who was a Blackfoot warrior, befriended a white man by the name of James Willard Schultz. My great-grandfather would tell Schultz about war parties, hunting parties and different things the Blackfoot had done. As Schultz wrote these stories he would place himself in my great-grandfather's moccasins. Schultz was a drunkard who capitalized on my great-grandfather's exploits. This information was given to me by my great aunt Agnes Guardipee Augare."

As I drive out through the little town of Browning, I glance over and see a Piegan man skinning a deer on his backporch. The carcass is hung by its heels, and the skin is mostly off, and there in good clear daylight is the pink of the Belly Buttes, the pink-white, the mottled quartzy pink striated with red. At last, the solid image, the regardless thing-itself, behind the syllables.

Great Falls by dark.

South Platte Points

THE JULY MORNING is so foggy along the South Platte that walking the river bottom is strangely apprehensive, like moving through a very dark and unfamiliar room. Visibility is barely ten yards. Meadowlark song jabs out from the fog-mist on all sides; overhead, the *chacks* of unseen blackbirds passing by.

The stubby light lends the morning an expectancy and gives the botany in particular a new cast. The green-blue of prickly poppy, the summer milkweed apparatus, the young sage—all take on a modest brilliance. I can hear the river running a few feet off, a large invisible thing. Crows in the distance sound nervous with the shrunken vista. But the Lark sparrows seem to like the subdued light, sing on and on from off in the shrouded wings.

It is a hike of short, well-considered steps. I am about to stop and turn back when a male Blue grosbeak darts out from the fog and lands for several uncertain seconds on a low limb. Darkest lapis. If kings or potentates still presented specimens of high regard from their native soil to royalty afar, a cage of Blue grosbeaks—

lapis and chocolate—would be paramount from this quarter of the continent.

~

I visit the South Platte more and more frequently of late, drop in somewhere between Denver and the Colorado-Nebraska line. Sometimes I drive out from the city to escape the heat and fumes and the constant needling of the public printed word of which I am by nature destined to read each syllable. Sometimes I get off Interstate 76, tired of the highspeed drone, and seek a halfhour of shade and respite along its banks. Other days I simply feel the need for riverine companionship and drive out to one of the state-owned public areas on the river (there are six or eight good ones between Ft. Lupton and Julesburg) to hike a mile or two and see, simply, what's going on.

This is *not* the stretch of the South Platte where Eisenhower fished. To many eyes it is the unglamorous part of the river, flowing best it can through heavily farmed and quarried plainsland. But it is buffered, mercifully, along most of its course by cottonwood bottoms and a narrow habitat of good old fashioned brush and tangle and willow brake and chokecherry amid the mixed mongrel grasses and a sprinkling of old bedsprings and rotting appliances and flood junk. It is a dense enough bottom to retain the cachet of river as

Otherplace, as a distinctive ecology, especially within the high plains and most decisively within the often bruising agribusiness on its flanks.

My affection and respect for the South Platte of the plains are fairly recent. I have always appreciated the simple strength of its flow and the comfort of its raggedy presence. But more and more I admire it as one of the powerful, easily overlooked assets of the region, as one of the most gifted of oxygen-bearing givens of this part of the world. Maybe the growing affection has something to do with the unpredictability of the river. It is always different; each time I return it seems the channel has shifted; the islets have slightly altered; the cottonwood skeletons in midstream moved a bit downriver, as if they changed positions during sleep; another chunk of sandy bank has collapsed into the current, with mink tracks already on it.

But any season there is always the good murmur and chortle of water, the oldest moving thing, and sooner or later a flock of crows in the neighborhood. The crows, of course, know the river best of all, keep a daily perspicacious eye on it through its permutations and adjustments. Over decades, they chronicle the great gristle of its continuity.

~

November 25. Near Sedgwick: The muted early winter colors are on the bottomlands—mouse-gray, dun, copper in the trees and shrubs. The frosted tawny of the dead grasses. I walk over to the Platte through an open plantation of mature cottonwoods with the buckbrush below them showing that evasive purple-brown of its winter tone. There is still a trace of fine floury snow on the ground, and even a thin edging of ice in the quiet riverside pools. Barkless snags protrude from the main current every thirty or forty yards. When the clouds open and the sun strengthens even an iota, the willow clumps on the sandbars brighten, intensify to luminous and cheery rust-orange.

It is quiet, even cozy when the sun is out; just the pleasant babble of the left bank below me. A killdeer in the distance. Then, beyond the river, there is movement. Three crows, it is, flying casually upstream, then another half dozen come into view, weaving in almost lolling flight through the cottonwood grove. Then more, and more, until there is a strung-out flock of sixty birds moving along at leisure, at ease, silent. It is a formidable, dignified presence and procession through the winter calm. I watch them, in their unhurried aplomb, until they disappear upriver.

Crow flocks often have that feel of communal languor, almost a magesterial languor projecting both wisdom and conscious pride. Some of the huge flocks of yore one reads about must have been astonishing to see. Arthur Bent informs us that western crows colonize in far greater numbers than eastern American crows. He writes of flocks and roosts of 200, even 500 thousand birds in the southern plains around the turn of the century. Oklahoma in the 1930s claimed a winter crow population of almost four million, and "bombing the roosts" was a standard tactic to protect pecan orchards and other crops. There are reports of 40 thousand birds destroyed in night bombings in Texas; 26 thousand in a roost bombed in Oklahoma. A black shambles.

Any gregarious creature-motion like a crow flock operating within its flexible range is eye-catching, thought-catching—the mechanism and the mutuality of it all—and with crows, those sharpest of eyes, those talkers and chroniclers, it is moreso. When I picture large flocks ranging the prairie rivers I remember, somehow, the distribution maps of the huge bison herds on the Great Plains of old in Mari Sandoz's *The Buffalo Hunters:* the Republican River herd, the Arkansas River herd, and so on. That fierce many-bodied singlemindedness moving up and down those streams.

When I sleep in Denver there is a small urban crow flock that appears each morning just seconds after daybreak, gradually emerges one or two birds at a time from behind the tall 1st Avenue buildings, assembles, and makes its way in a hedging, sleepy rhythm through the crimson dawnlight, southerly, high over the apartment building, to Cherry Creek, where it drops down to drink at the sandbars and sun in the riparian trees. Each morning I am awake early enough to watch, they move in a near identical formation from roost to morning river. Like the sun-crow in old Chinese mythology, making its daily implacable flight across the sky.

It is only fitting to think of them, or it, as direct descendants of a long-established pre-Denver flock, a gene pool relatively stable and contented in its place for a long, long time, going on about its age-old business in a steady way, optimistically indifferent to the settlement and growth of the city—a more varied and highly spiced food supply the major point of interest. As it is only proper to consider the indigenous genealogy of the birds of Mesa Verde: the nearly indestructible genetic shard of those calls and songs over centuries amid the piñons.

Walking past the Cherry Creek crows later in the day I admire them as they feed on the grass of the park or preen in the streamside trees, admire them as one might admire wolfhounds or Percherons in clover— their trim tailoring, the cut of their jib.

~

We went out to the river near 88th Avenue, the north edge of Denver, to check the wintering ducks both on the Platte and on the city ponds just west. Looking for

Old Squaws and Barrow's goldeneye—cold weather specialties—among the large flocks that ply between the fenced-off ponds and the river. And after a few minutes of glassing the gently bobbing rafts of mixed species, there was a Barrow's, in high tuxedo-sheen, with that odd, excessive profile, the protruding forehead remindful of a certain high school teacher's husband.

The December morning was chilly and cloudless, cold enough that the power plant complex in the north-central city emitted a massive compound column of steam that rose high above, formed a cumulus mushroom head that eventually lost shape and drifted westerly toward the mountains with a kind of inarguable, unavoidable Niagara beauty.

And scorching August days uninoculated boys of derring-do still swim in the Platte, up at the confluence, in the pools at the mouth of Cherry Creek.

~

Third week of April. Downstream from Snyder.

A band of Yellowrumps works slowly through the big cottonwoods, feeding at leisure among the full blossom catkins. A balmy, sunny morning. When the warblers sing it is precisely as desultory and unrushed as their foraging. These mature cottonwood groves along the Platte, as along many other streams, stand as grand emblems and expression of the western rivers, especially on the plains. They are the *fruits* of these flows, and a stream without them, like the upper Niobrara or the buzzcut middle Arkansas, is a whimpering thing. After years of dawdling in their presence I have notebooks full of adjectives on their behalf: Elephantine and mastodonic; antediluvian; tangle-haired; Delphian and myopic; counter-redwood; fey and fatidic; Shivaesque. ... The list goes on.

Any full-scale grove of them is a wonder of secret gregarious power. Substantial boles three and four feet through, flouting all conventional notions of symmetry and form, it's as if they gaze continually off into the sky in hopes that no one will notice them, that they might be left alone to live out their unassuming century.

To stand within such an open grove is a floating-world pleasure; but then to strike out and walk a lengthy river grove is such a heady experience that I have wanted for some time now to film that odd sensation of strolling slowly through the big widely spaced savannah trees, midwinter or pre-leaf spring, to catch the way the interlocking visual planes work, the nearer trees "moving" straight-faced with the spectator, the mid-distance and far ones shifting in lesser degrees. In sum, it creates an effect of almost comical planetary motion and relations, of a stately, balletic procession that dances back and forth between a choreographed formality and preposterous happenstance. There are film-worthy groves in abundance along the South Platte near Fort Morgan and Brush; along the Moreau and the Cheyenne rivers in South Dakota; on the North Platte where Horse Creek enters it; beside the upper Missouri; and many more.

This stretch of river has of course altered since my last visit: a portion of bank-ledge has fallen in, taking a section of fence with it, and a new antler of fallen tree has positioned itelf near shore, making a brand new eddy. Today again the Platte seems whimsical, a Coyote of a river, full of headlong foolishness, rambunctious false starts and pie-eyed deadends, and a little Get-in-Dutch trickery. (It was sheer coincidence that the first time I remarked this constant metamorphosis of the river was at the bridge just outside Ovid, Colorado.) On the far side, someone has deposited scrap concrete and an old car—an early '60s aqua and white Ford Fairlane—nose down in the river, trying to stabilize the bank.

But my affection for the South Platte grows. I consider the run from Denver to Julesburg a 250-mile cottonwood grove, a long, thin, hard-pressed grove. Sometimes frumpy, often ragged, yet dauntless in its way, and always oxygen-bearing. Its wide valley from Atwood and Sterling on out and the on-running hills above, all the way to Ovid, Sedgwick, on to Ogallala, make the highways—6, then 138—distinguished roads. The crows escort the river all the way; once in Nebraska, the cranes drop in now and again to lend a hand.

Most sizable cottonwood groves are comprised of a single generation of trees of about the same size, a fact explained by the young trees' need for full sunlight; they are incapable of competing with other species in a shaded understory. Either they all make it, or none do. And when a grove dies of old age at seventy-five or 100 years, it is replaced by a complete new sibling cohort.

It gives the riverine prairie groves a familial, herdlike appearance and a feeling of bemused purposeful measure. Even a single matriarchal/patriarchal tree of good girth conveys that heavy, clear-eyed sense of ancient thick-skinned witness, the mute testimony one finds most often in mountains or buttes—the sensation of *Panorama well-anchored.* But a thriving adult grove is like the chorus in the old Greek plays. Wise, wizened, barnacled as whales, full of deep savannah calm.

I happened across the cohort-inscape one early-summer day ten years ago along the White River in South Dakota. I was hiking with my friend Fitzpatrick on a remote section somewhere downstream from the village of Interior. Eventually, on a long narrow sandbar at one edge of the White, I looked down and realized the entire dune-bar, perhaps twenty yards long, was covered with four-inch infant cottonwoods, delicate seedlings, fresh-leaved and fluttering in the breeze. It was a nursery of a forest. The generational front and cohesion, the upsurge and phalanx of it, was there in symphonic strength, and I knelt a good while watching the little red-stemmed grove rollick and quake.

~

Late September. Out beyond Brush.

This morning I was out along the river early, the grasses held heavy dew. I was walking upstream, with the low sun at my back, when a birdcall stopped me, turned me, and looking east I noticed a number of spider webs deployed in the grasses, shining brilliantly in the morning rays. I walked back and looked from the other side; they were virtually invisible from that angle. I began to retrace my steps, carefully, toward the sun, and there were more: fifteen or twenty of them at hand, ranging in size from three to nine inches in diameter, all of elegant and at the moment luminous design. Stepping off to one side and shading my eyes—make it fifty. Make it a hundred!

I began to inspect the array. On some of the larger foot-wide webs I found the artisan at rest, a formidable spider about an inch long, a white body striped with yellow, toasting in the 7:30 sun. And down low in the grama grass, I discovered small webs, quick and offhand, or perhaps novice efforts, hardly two inches across. And soggy, broken ones, drooping and torn like old fishing nets. There were webs of some sort every two, or four, or six feet across the bottom. I suspected the tiny understated ones might be practice webs, or even exercises spun from boredom. But no—each one of them had a tiny dot in its center, the size of a poppy seed, and when I touched one of them with a twig it fell like a piece of chaff, then awakened and began to move up the web: a tiny spider, of course.

Then I quit and stood up and looked against the sun. The whole field was full of the things, mined with them. What had appeared a rather stodgy uninteresting bottomland was in fact full of craft and intricate design, rich with artifacts primal as medieval weaponry, or the centuries-old mossbacked stone fish impoundments on the Atlantic coast of the Isle d'Oléron.

Later I drove up the valley, hugging the river as closely as the meager dirt roads allowed, crossing and recrossing. There were still a few cicadas and other trillers in the trees, and fox squirrels sunned high in the cottonwoods.

At midday a fortuitous turn over a rickety bridge brought me into a Platte-side hamlet of maybe 500 souls. It was an ordinary enough village, breathing easy with Fall, but something—maybe the few extra clusters of people here and there, or the kids and dogs all loping in the same direction through the earthen streets—hinted that this was not a run-of-the-mill Saturday.

After a quick lunch in the car, I drove through town, away from the main highway, and followed a pair of boys on bikes to a tiny turn-of-the-century school-house. Behind it, nestled like a bright jewel in the dusty school yard, was a small well-groomed football field. Around the edges men were placing yard markers and readying equipment. A few early spectators were filing in past the ticket takers, among them two farm women who told me the game was between this school and another fifty miles north, that kickoff was at 1:00, and, best of all, that it was six-man.

Serendipity on the Platte. I dug a jacket out of the trunk and walked back to the field. The wind had picked up and swung around to the north. Cars and pickups were edging close around one corner of the playing field; corn grew tall within a few feet of the far side and the far end. Six cheerleaders were chanting along one sideline; for whatever reason, the visiting team didn't have any. The hometown squad of thirteen was warming up and running plays. The local quarterback was having trouble with his passes; after a wild off-target throw, you could hear his frustrated "Gee-aw."

I had already decided to side with the visitors, ten boys from a town I knew from prairie rambles, a town in the midst of federal grasslands so high and dry and lonesome it made you think of distance by the snake-length and luxury as getting in out of the wind; a region that made even this river village seem promising. These were ranchers' sons, whose nightly football practice meant long drives and extra work for someone at home.

It was all comfortably familiar. In my home county in Ohio in the early '60s, before the baby-boomers achieved puberty and school consolidation became the rage, six-man was still viable. Those eighty- by forty-yard fields are all elementary-school playgrounds by now, or parking lots, but in those days they drew people in pickup trucks from miles around on Saturday afternoons. I remember the crowds, small ones of course, people gathered in little groups, chatting the way they do on the sidewalk after church. There were sunburned faces you saw only two or three times a year along the sidelines. Few people sat; the idea was to saunter along the field, renewing acquaintances.

The coaches always seemed to be men of a special cut—loud, solid and knowing, with enough rustic flair and vocabulary to get the whole operation off the ground and keep it there. Most of those I recall were legendary outdoorsmen, coon hunters or hound trainers, men who knew what to do with their whiskey autumn nights when the dogs struck a trail. And there was always a herd of Holsteins grazing just beyond one end zone.

Now the cheerleaders were trying to outshout the Platte valley wind and they were mostly failing. By kickoff time there were probably 150 people standing around. There were two fifteen-foot bleacher sections of six to eight planks each. In these sat mothers with their infants; the sidelines filled up with men wearing baseball caps or battered Stetsons. One official was mingling with the crowd; another was tossing a ball in the air and whistling "You Are My Sunshine."

It was American football in crystalline miniature. The spectators were on their feet, then the ball was in the air. It was just one kickoff of many at that moment, but for a split second I felt a surge of deep autumn-Saturday sadness. Six boys, averaging 145 pounds, in a frail huddle under a wide, cold sky bathed in cornfield light had my hair on end.

Not that the football as played was any more primitive than many smalltown eleven-man versions. On the contrary, there were moments of classic six-man, those tight covey-bursts of speed and execution that call to mind the best of basketball. On this particular day, the air-borne variations seemed endless. Single plays incorporating a pitch, a reverse, and a country-mile pass were the rule rather than the exception.

No matter that the ballcarriers for the most part ran standing straight up and that the tackling was often above the waist. It was snappy, almost cavalier football. If there was any quaintness about the game, it was imposed by rural necessity: No matter at which end of the field a touchdown was scored, the points-after were kicked at the east end so the ball wouldn't disappear in the cornfield to the west.

By halftime the home team was leading 27–0. Most spectators hurried to their cars to crack a thermos of coffee and warm up. Only the elementary-school boys playing their own raggle-taggle scrimmage in the end zone ignored the cold breeze from Wyoming. At the end of the third quarter it was 35–0 and getting worse. My grasslands team couldn't take it in from the five, and I gave up.

Driving home, back toward the mountains, I turned the radio on and then the heater for the first time this season. Early scores were trickling in from the east coast. But I kept thinking about the miniature game I had left. I hoped the visitors were able to get some points on the board in the fourth, but I doubted it. I hadn't seen the dropkick I'd hoped to, but that was probably asking a bit much; one might never see a dropkick again.

I felt mildly bad for the high prairie boys. True, they were outmuscled slightly and seemed to tire early. And they were playing far from home, of course. They appeared to have trouble with their footing; I doubt that their home field had turf as lush and dense as that well-watered valley town's.

And maybe the corn had something to do with it. Maybe those seven-foot walls of corn on two sides induced a sort of claustrophobia in a team used to nothing taller than buffalo grass, prickly pear, and yucca. Maybe that was it.

A Pair of Canyons

THE PRICKLY PEARS across Las Animas County bloom so bright this June — brilliant masses of waxy yellow and bougainvillea pink against the wet-green vernal prairie — the whole region has the look of a vast Decoration Day cemetery or borderless, boundless fiesta. Flowers as startlingly incongruous on their humble cactus as the fancy mushrooms that spring from horse droppings. The land steadily rises, inexorably up from the Arkansas River valley, steels itself through cholla-covered slopes and cedared ridges with red cattle grazing among them. It is a solitary ascension; on a good map, windmills outnumber other structures in Las Animas and Baca counties four to one. A lone ibis blinks in a grassy puddle.

There was nothing open in the village of Kim, Colorado, no store, no cafe, no gas. I drove around the back streets in search of a person to ask about the minimal roads into the Comanche National Grasslands, roads to Cottonwood and Carrizo canyons. There was no one in sight except two lads intently repairing a playwagon. I finally found a man leaving his house and consulted him before driving east from town on the gravel road and off into the titanic spaces.

Springtime without trees has its own shoelace-level joy. I stopped twice when I got out into the plains and stepped out to listen for Cassin's sparrow song, hoping for a jolt of that spring music, but the wind was too strong. If anything was singing within earshot of the road, the notes were cut to a thin northbound ribbon. People in La Junta, where the hollyhocks were knee-high, talked everywhere about the wind, as did people in Lamar yesterday. It has been on the prowl for a while now. So I watched for Cassin's kingbird instead. In an hour, after more than one false turn on the lookalike anonymous roads, I reached Cottonwood Canyon.

It is my first visit and the scale of the place is surprising. A northern part of the extensive Black Mesa rough-country, it is a canyon remindful of some of the smaller side canyons at Mesa Verde, with imposing rock cliffs at its upper edges and dark cedars on its steep slopes. Cottonwood Creek itself, the mastermind, is a slow thing today, lazing from puddle to puddle through willow clumps and cattails.

I park and walk the canyon road a mile and back, then out a small tributary canyon to an overgrown cabin site beside a spring. It has a dilapidated milchcow yard and a skillfully built stone cistern in a breezeway to catch the spring water and cool the milk pails, and a noteworthy roof of two-inch thick cement—cement as severe extension of adobe. Upstream on Cottonwood Creek I hear an Ash-throated flycatcher and then an Eastern phoebe. An orange butterfly wends down the creek, flying below the cutbank to avoid the pesky wind.

There is a family group at the small picnic ground where I parked. The children have found distraction in hauling large rocks to the bridge and throwing them into the stream. In a short while the two adult men are taken with the notion and join them. They go off up the slope and find bigger and bigger rocks and lug them to the bridge and drop them over and wait for the concussive splash. An absurdist glee is building. The two women are over watching by now. The one fellow has just come out of the brush perspiring heavily with a chunk of stone the size of a peck basket. When it hits the creek we all laugh uproariously.

Cottonwood Creek can probably appreciate the lively diversion for a quarter hour. It seems uninspired, needs a good stiff rain, eagles with lightning. Its farflung canyon with the devoted local clientele has an awkward parochial ambiance that both piques and annoys. We are lulled, we are taking it too much for granted. I try to concentrate on its bird's eye implications, its receptive southfacing bearing, open like a good harbor to austral things: calming sun in winter, all that Comancherian, Chihuahuan, equatorial silence and flow.

John Cassin lived from 1813–1869. He was apparently an avid indoorsman. He was ornithology curator and taxonomist at the Philadelphia Academy of Natural Sciences, where he uncrated and classified and shelved bird specimens sent to him from all over the outer world. I don't know that he ever got out west at all, but he named three prominent birds of the inland west after himself, it seems (as well as another Pacific seabird): the sparrow, the kingbird, and the high country Cassin's finch. It seems like a lot, even for a dedicated scientist; it's more than Audubon or Alexander Wilson, the great field men, can show. Cassin's kingbird could just as readily be called the Highland kingbird, or the Yucca kingbird. And the sparrow, with its delicate but firm habitat preferences, might be known as the Shortgrass sparrow or the Highplains sparrow, the Llano, or the Bluesky sparrow. ... Then, beyond the creek, a Blue grosbeak alights, peering, in a scrub oak—the third of the trip, I saw two over on the Cimarron yesterday.

After lunch I drive downcanyon. The steep-walled valley gradually widens into luxuriant meadows, and then into agriculture. After six miles Cottonwood Creek joins Carrizo Creek just below a well-kept bridge. At that point I turn north and follow the latter stream for a couple of miles, then off into prairie uplands again. All the human structures hereabouts are built of the good local ochre-colored stone.

A Pair of Canyons

I stop and walk out through a yucca field, all the plants in full creamy blossom. In some places they grow so profusely it is impossible to walk through them. Yucca groves; yucca droves. The flowers are both handsome and, up close, lacking, resembling a crude, would-be, "oceanfloor" lily. It's still too windy on the grasslands to hear sparrow song, so I drive on toward Carrizo Canyon. I stop to look at a dead owl (a Barn owl) on the road. When I open the door and lean out to turn the carcass over a dozen inch-long red and black carrion beetles charge the car.

I spend the afternoon at the little trailhead/picnic area on the edge of Carrizo Canyon. This canyon is a smaller thing by far than Cottonwood, but it has a certain intensity of its own: Massive sharp-edged chunks of stone lie about the lower slopes, snapped off and strewn like cooking-chocolate. It has deep dragonfly pools and basins amid the ochre cliff jumble and dusty equisetum stands.

I sit there for several hours. It is a soundless spot, except for distant cattle bawling and a cuckoo jugging down at streamside. On a far hill I find something through the binoculars that looks like a rusty left-behind river barge or dredge heating up to griddle point in the afternoon sun.

I stroll up the creek and circle out among the grasses. Swallows have come out there, too, from their stream-side shelter, to hawk above the prairie and its flowers.

Headwaters of the Cimarron! An open-armed place for sure, a place for no small thoughts.

I open a can of beans. The wind blows part of my supper right off the table—the bagel, then the tomato.

~

In a small high plains town 250 miles to the north a tableau of Passion Defused, unique and brief as a snowflake, congealed this afternoon. In front of the county courthouse, beside a brick-edged bed of long-legged tulips, stand a deputy sheriff and two disparate civilians in handcuffs. One of the latter is a gangly teenaged boy; the other is a bull-necked man about sixty wearing Atlantic-edge clothing and a clipped Prussian-style mustache, salt and pepper, no egg.

An aged chap sits on a shaded parkbench a few yards to one side, along a border of the courthouse green. Bone weary of the gruesome present, he has for some time now arranged his daily meditation such that he spends most of his hours in the period just preceding the first World War. Each afternoon, with varying difficulty and infinite clearings of the throat, he reaches that sunny carefree decade, spirals determinedly up and up, and hangs in suspended revery there for a happy while, with his eyes half closed, in a cool, lilac-scented yard with a huge long-dead dog named Richard, a toy tractor, and a sleepy white goose.

A Pair of Canyons

The man with the clipped mustache is a butterfly collector of the most serious type. He had rolled his nets and left his Staten Island home a month before and embarked on a transcontinental field trip with the purpose of filling in certain painful gaps in his specimen trays. Two weeks later he arrived in this eastern Colorado town at lunchtime and as he ate a Denver omelet he saw the boy idling on a streetcorner. Moments later he had hired him as a guide to take him into a little-traveled public tract of the county to seek out a rare and heavily protected butterfly in its sole locale. The boy would know which dirt roads led anywhere and which didn't, would save him hours, if not days.

That afternoon they drove out into the area, a rough terrain of palomino breaks and barren hillocks, and set up their camp: an ample wall tent, folding chairs and a miniature table with a tuzzy-muzzy of prairie flowers on it. Then they went off up the hill with the nets.

They were there two days. A Forest Service ranger had spotted the tent the first afternoon, checked it through field glasses from an escarpment afar. When he saw it again the next morning, he decided to go over and have a look—the place was a notorious suicide site for star-crossed lovers from the mountain towns a short drive to the west. The bottle of Goldwasser and the small top-quality safe chained in the back of the Range Rover made him instantly suspicious.

He lay in wait behind a cedar wall through the warm afternoon, and came again next morning, early enough to see the two leave with their nets and he knew what they were after. When they returned at midday the ranger was there, stepped out from the cedars as the boy was pouring a jug of water over his head and the mustached man had just opened an elegant enameled box that resembled a cigarette case and held his prized specimens. He had covered some ground, that was both obvious and touching. His box held a Bay Checkerspot from San Mateo county, an Uncompahgre fritillary from a valley in the Rockies, even an Emerald dragon-fly from a bog just west of Toledo.

So the ranger took them in. The man from New York assumed from the first instant a demeanor of im-pervious contempt for the preposterous situation, its petty bureaucratic insistence. He went through it all with a mental sneer and a faultless unctuous diction.

Outside the courthouse this afternoon they all stood waiting for the sheriff's van to take them into Denver for the paperwork. A freckling June sunlight was on them, and for half a minute the tableau vivant rose around and within them, a byproduct of the day, as they each harked off in half-thought, floated off from the others until even the circumstantial mooring of the group dissolved, and they took on the eyeless look of Grecian statues.

The deputy stared vacantly at the upper story of an empty building across the street where a blind drooped askew; he pictured himself lovingly washing his car before supper. The boy looked off at nothing in the eastern sky, held up his handcuffed hands to test a quiet pimple on his chin. The mustached man faced south-southwest. He envisioned himself for an instant back in California one week before, smoking a fine tight cigarillo in the shade of a eucalyptus. A pretty housefly lit on his safari vest lapel.

Hidatsa Traces

I WAS DRIVING BETWEEN Marmath and Rhame, North Dakota. It was early evening, the buttes were casting long shadows in the late sun. There, high up on the Little Missouri River, I remembered for a moment a Thomas Hardy poem, "The Bridge of Lodi." I remembered that it rhymed with "toady." The poem recounts in dutiful quatrains Hardy's visit to the Italian site of a substantial clash between Napoleon's army and Austrian forces. The English even had a folk tune about the battle. Hardy hummed and whispered it as he lingered on the historic bridge and ambled avuncularly through the town. But to his amazement no one about the place—shopkeepers, strollers—was even aware of the events that rattled their campaniles less than a century before.

I remembered that poem because I was in butte country and they were taking on that homesick evening-sun look, and I was thinking, I suppose, of erosion and atrophy and wash-away and large, charged events vanishing.

Here on the northern plains, if one were of a mind to cache something precious, treasure or crucial cultural lode, sought to stow it, bestow it, safe from flood and plow, daily shuffle, bloodhound and truffle hog—they would do well to pack it up a butte and leave it there, high above.

Indomitable places draw primordial notions. Difficult, untrammeled places house and shelter the talisman and nurturing myth, the taproot metaphysics of any geography; shelter them as much as is ever possible from the blow-out and evaporation of time and blood and thunder. They survive, it occurred to me that evening, not so much because of their specific contents but by virtue of their particular placement-in-landscape, their *inlay*.

And meanwhile the meadowlarks were having a strong final say from the fenceposts.

~

The western Dakota territory is an archipelago of buttes. From virtually any point between the forks of the Cheyenne River and the Canadian border there is visible, in some quadrant of the horizon, a butte, and often several, rising, beckoning, heavy with spoor. Active, catalytic features of the landscape, they "move" as one views them from different perspectives, pronouncing, apportioning. A single well-made butte dominates its surrounding terrain for as long as it can be seen. On first view it establishes itself as the potent place, the unclaimable, untillable place of thrust, and from all angles, in all its changing aspects and lights and innuendo, it holds as a magnetic referent above the plains.

The moment one enters North Dakota's southwest corner the buttes are there in a constant flurry of knobs and red-speckled pyramids and grassy knolls (the word "butte" comes from the French for "knoll") of much firmer form than the muddy bulges of southeastern Montana. Approaching the town of Bowman, I watch the Twin Buttes take their stations, a close-set pair of remarkable beauty and twinship from fifteen miles away—and then, in town, find their lee sides afflicted with homes and antennae and a large BOWMAN in whitewashed stone. Talbot Butte, east of the village, is a dominant feature in that quarter, a handsome flat-topped grassy butte of good lines and form. But I am stopping at Bowman in search of larger things.

The next morning I drive north from town. Six miles out I pull over and wipe off the binoculars to look at White Butte sprawling on the northern skyline. White Butte is indeed a major presence, a long rough-and-tumble leviathan presence, a butte of the lumbering, several-parted sort, a gangly bulwark quite different from the neat table-topped vertical entities common down in South Dakota. Through the field glasses it has a hot, barnacled appearance, rough with snow-like colloid outcroppings and upper-level badland breaks shimmering in the heat.

By my calculations White Butte is the "Rosebud Butte" of the Hidatsa peoples, the landmark staking the outpost southwestern edge of traditional Hidatsa territory and one of the four imposing "Buffalo Spirit Places" emanating the very life-source of the human tribes. Raw and powerful, it hangs above the grain- and grasslands like thunderheads above a county fair.

And there are others titillating on the horizon: a leading cedar-lipped actor just peeking from far behind the foreground hills—maybe one of the Rainy Buttes marked on the map—and, straight east, a neat set shaky in the haze, an extensive central ridge flanked by two flat-topped outriders.

They have all borne many names, no doubt. Always significant compass points, these North Dakota buttes became much more for the Hidatsa. Layered and layered again with story and myth, the buttes emerged as stanchions of Hidatsa presence on the upper Missouri River and its watershed, binding the Hidatsa people to their land; explaining their distant past; anchoring their daily ways of life; standing ready as pillars to entertain their supplications. A drive across North Dakota nonchalantly passes buttes of noble lineage and often heroic drama, points touched and charred by preternatural lightning.

Now they sit high and dry and largely forgotten among the badlands and wheat-world, left stranded by the sudden contraction of Hidatsa lands in the mid-nineteenth century, left hanging in foreign hands. I am here this week, with a good map and a book of the old stories near at hand as Baedekker, to dust them off a little and view them for a moment in their rightful light. To cast an eye on those high points looming sharp and rock-solid from the myth fogs.

When the Hidatsa groups entered the upper Missouri region (estimates range from 1200 to 1500 A.D.) they needed first of all to negotiate and construct a mythic webbing and foundation for their presence there. It is a universal need for new arrivals in strange lands; for shamanistic peoples it involves appeasing the spirits of the region, asking their permission to stay, to thrive and not be crushed and spit out by the unknown territory and its mysterious psychoecology. Boundaries for the immigrants must be established. The spiritual places must be located, assessed, and scrupulously named.

For the Hidatsa this process was accomplished through a complex series of sacred myths and their de-volved ceremonies known collectively as the Earth-naming rites. Way back when, shortly after the Hidatsa arrived on the Missouri, a captive boy named Raven Necklace, after performing a number of heroic deeds on behalf of his adopted tribe, was visited by a formidable spirit owl, who instructed the boy in building a buffalo corral in the Missouri valley (a revolutionary food-procuring technique) and then informed him of the Earthnaming protocol, wherein various spirits of the new Hidatsa terrain would visit the boy in dreams and teach him the secrets and the songs of the land: "They will tell you the names of these high hills. There will be a great deal of memorizing." And over the ensuing winter the spirits came to Raven Necklace, each from their respective home-butte in the outlying Hidatsa lands, and coached him in the vital fluency, the songs and rituals and ceremonial bundles connected to their particular powers. Then, with the authority configuration grasped and schematized, the buffalo cleared as a foodsource, and the vast land flagged with Hidatsa names, the people stirred, understood, took root.

Anthropologists can point to very similar processes for the Navajo, the Omaha, the Cheyenne, when those peoples moved into new domains. And the tightly braided, topography-based blend of religion, political rationale, and cultural history is remindful of the native Australian peoples, their millennia-long cadastral dreamings. Both traditions share the irreplaceable knowledge that the secret heart and law of the earth is not only discovered, but maintained and nourished through earth-grounded song and tale. The land is seen as a narrative interacting with the human imuge earthlodge inhabited by dogs, fierce uncowed dogs possesed of chthonic powers capable, among other things, of driving humans insane. They dance the dog dance carrying their removable heads in their hands. Later in the many-tiered myth, one of the Hidatsa-pup boys who has mastered supernatural powers in his own right returns to the butte and tames the dangerous dog sorcerers (the "Crazy Dogs") and carries off a new bride at the same time.

There was more to come for Dog Den. An eon or so later, Sun himself, angered by the temerity and improvident hunting practices of the upstart humans, chose to imprison all the animal species on the northern plains and drove them en masse into Dog Den and sealed the door and the smokehole. It took considerable doing and major assistance from First Creator himself to free the creatures and save the chastised Hidatsas from starvation.

And as the sundown colors deepen, the earthlodge analogy is brilliantly apt and beautiful. I sit on the car hood and watch for a while. The broad-shouldered height and dominance of the butte is more obvious now; it is the major landmark this side of the Missouri River for a long long way. There are three or four radio towers at the grassy rounded summit. Its gentle flanks are streaked dark with brushy runnels trickling ash and oak draws. The butte has the complex life-surge of a marsh or a giant redwood.

agination, an "artifact of intellect" to be studied and read.

After an hour of sizing White Butte from various aspects, I continue north and spend all afternoon hiking on the Little Missouri National Grasslands. Next day I drive to the mouth of Heart River, where the Heart empties into the Missouri just below the city of Mandan, North Dakota. I pull off at a wide spot overlooking the confluence. Half-cut hayfields lay below on the jut of land between the two rivers. Canada geese glean the mowed sections, keeping a sharp eye on the heavy route 1806 traffic at my back. It is a cool, cloudy day. This semiscenic, rather busy edge-of-town spot, according to the Hidatsa and their Mandan neighbors, is the precise site of the creation of the earth in its present form.

This is the place where First Creator and Lone Man, likeable protohuman wanderers, encountered each other and after a rigorous genealogical discussion and a round of protobanter decided to make the chaotic earth inhabitable. First Creator opted to design the land south of the Missouri, Lone Man that to the north. The former built a terrain of great variety, full of hills and mountains, coulees and breaks: a good well-watered land. Lone Man's effort north of the river was less attractive; he laid out the trying monotone visible today up around Minot, a region the Hidatsa asserted was to be held in reserve against the time the good lands were tainted. To be held in reserve, especially, for the rumored coming of the Caucasians and their plodding herds.

When the solid earth was completed and the leftover dirt piled into a pointed butte (certainly one of those within sight of where I stand), the two protagonists sat down to rest and smoke their pipes together. "This will be the center," First Creator announced. "This will be the Heart of the World."

Down below, to my left, a pair of aluminum canoes put in to Heart River—Heart-of-the-World River—and set off bobbing and thudding toward the mouth. Geese watch, and motorcycles roar by. This is a difficult place to begin. It is public and distracting, hard to burn through. But we have checked in, and an oriole sings. And what is to be done after all? A half-hearted snapshot? There is an inelastic limit-of-reach looking pastward that is one of the great (and certainly preservational) helplessnesses. How much can tea-sippers in the Fertile Crescent care for all that story off behind *them*?

All I can think to mutter is "May sleek sage grow in your ruins" as I climb back in the car.

A tough, tractionless place to begin. But I cross the Missouri and drive through Bismarck—the Golden Dragon, the Jade Garden, the Hong Kong restau-

rants—and strike north. In an hour I st[o] range of buttes off to the east, off toward [t] Tuttle or Hurdsfield. On the map they ar[e] Prophet Mountains; I figure they com[e] down, the "Opposite Buttes"—the south stone of old Hidatsa territory. From [V] where I paused day before yesterday t[o] grassy hills, thence north to the Turtle M[the Canadian border (the northeast poin[t] west-southwest to a butte the Hidatsa calle[d] (located just north of the mouth of the Yel[traditional Hidatsa lands within this parall[cluded some 30 thousand square miles w[i] river at its core.

I continue north and begin a skyline wa[Den Butte. Slowly and implacably it rises. [slowly realize that that subtly imposing, [massive bulge lifting among the lesser co[thing itself. The nearer I drive, cutting off o[to circle it and catch its eastern aspect, the c[mension becomes: Now this is a wilder, [thing. And suddenly, watching it form [brightening late afternoon western sky, I [the giant domed earthlodge that the Hidats[a]

In the old days a Hidatsa woman gave b[pups. Not long after, the frisky litter led th[Dog Den Butte and they entered via the s[the top. The woman discovers the butte i[

Hidatsa Traces

I would like to hike up and watch the sunset from there near the erstwhile smokehole, crazy dogs or no. As I drive slowly by on the north side in the last light of day I spot an abandoned, ill-advised farmhouse cold and dumb way up near the top—the inhabitants no doubt run amok with dog fever and now gasping for breath somewhere far away. Then I head east and north to find a room for the night.

~

The following noon I make a commemoratory stop along the south shore of Devil's Lake. This is the site of the proto-Hidatsas' first topside camp after they emerged from underground, called up by First Creator from their netherworld, packing their horticultural goods and gear on their backs. And here beside Devil's Lake they rested. Bathed in cool water. Caught their breath and shaded their eyes to look about the new sky-topped world before commencing their mytho-historic wanderings that would eventually end on the Missouri. They would experience punitive celestial fire that scattered them into separate bands and a scourging celestial flood that drove the prudent among them to the lofty Square Buttes (along the Missouri fifteen or twenty miles north of Mandan), where they awaited the receding of the waters and climbed down to try again.

Devil's Lake is big, dignified water. Elder Hidatsas early this century claimed that the dead returned to this place to reside. The shore today is pleasant enough. The day is hot; Sioux families, the current residents of the Devil's Lake Sioux Reservation, wade in the finger-slapping surf. Wooded hills rise hard by on the south. Cormorants wait on whitened stumps, dive for sweet baby perch or walleye. As I stroll the shore, what I take for small flowers beside a mud puddle turn out to be dozens of lavender butterflies that scatter like a covey.

The weather has steadily warmed. At Devil's Lake I opt to escape the Dakota sun and drive a hundred miles northwest into the Turtle Mountains straddling the Manitoba border. They are more nearly hearty hills than mountains, but they carry enough arch to support a distinctly northern, sweet-shaded canopy of aspen and poplar and to hold chilly, beaver-creased lakes and millions of mosquitoes.

I rent a small waterless cabin near Lake Metigoshe. For two days I wash clothes and hang them to dry on bushes, cook several variants of near-naked spaghetti, and sip instant coffee in the shade of a saskatoon sapling outside the door. The popple forest surrounding, I note after a day and a half, has two and only two frequencies: The aspens are either vividly aflutter and shaking tambourine-like in the sun, or, with a difference sudden as the drawing of a venetian blind, they stand utterly, uncannily, still, poised, at the ready like dancers in the wings.

White pelican flocks circle lazily high above the lake; I get the feeling their eyes are closed. It is only July, but here and there an ash tree shows a twinge of yellow leaf. That might account for one dream episode I had that night: a brief segment with a sort of "speech frost" emerging from my mouth in conversation in the form of stylized golden aspen leaves. Later, same night, I dreamt I was looking curiously back over my shoulder, could see all the sleep of my life piled along the "road" like deep plowed snow. ...

The Turtle Mountains being a Hidatsa corner-marker, I browse a little each day in the book of myths and look off from high spots toward the south. I still experience an odd thrill when I read of this or that cosmic event placed off-handedly in our present gas station world: "This happened," one informant tells us, "about a mile south of Sanger, North Dakota." In one of the stories there is a lovely instance of myth unflappability, in reference to the first exploratory encounter between two disparate Hidatsa bands: "They [the newcomer group] said they would return in four days, but they didn't come back for four years."

The Hidatsa myths are many-pronged and densely overlapping in a way that reflects the early fragmentations and migrations of the various bands, the long uncertain wanderings and circlings back. The Awatixa band was the earliest to settle on the Missouri. Their oldest myths are set, accordingly, and well-plotted on that very stretch of the river north of the Heart's mouth. Many of their traditions concern the settling of that region.

The other branches of the tribe came later to the Missouri. They had spent an extra few generations wandering the plains to the east of the river. Their myths consequently hark more to that region—Devil's Lake and beyond—and recount adventures of exodus and trial out there. There are echoes and alternate readings and counterpoint discrepancies among the various tales. They sometimes sound like three or four versions of the same symphony being played simultaneously, full of crackle and unsynchronized blare—but with the same theme and motives nonetheless.

Once all the Hidatsa groups were on the Missouri, the myths eventually dovetailed and hybridized to form the complicated corpus that was recorded early this century. ... *They showed up one day four years later*—or forty, for that matter—with their stories streaming out behind.

After a good rest in the Turtle Mountain shade, I move back onto the plains, down through Minot and the "Lone Man flats" and on south. Soon Dog Den is there again, riding magisterially far off my left elbow. After crossing the big bay of Lake Sakakawea I drive west over the Missouri to Pick City and then south to the Knife River villages historic site, a cluster of one-time Hidatsa towns situated where the Knife joins the big river.

This is the solid-earth point of all this Hidatsa touring and mythic salvage. These villages are well documented and thoroughly excavated. Catlin and Bodmer painted them in the 1830s. Now, there is a shallow circular depression in the valley floor where each Hidatsa earthlodge stood, and an awkward summer melancholy to the place. The village sites appear as fragile and temporary as the pressed grass where a deer has bedded for a night. I suspect even the bone fragments scattered about were sown by federal rangers to distract relic lovers from the real thing.

But the rivers still flow, and I have two things I want to do on this visit. I eat an orange and then hike off to the north from the Big Hidatsa townsite, leaving the fenced-off mowed area and continuing another mile through the tall grass to view for a moment another fragrant relict: the subtle ruts and forkings of the centuries-old travois-worn trails approaching the village from upriver, cresting the skyline hills through a faint, grassgrown, gunsight notch.

And half an hour later I drive a couple of miles south and park again and walk to a second village site, the Awatixa town said to be the home of Sacajawea. This village is set directly on the edge of the present-day

Knife River and the stream has taken some of the site over the years, exposing a high, bison bone and midden studded bank. But what remains is a good place, quieter and more removed than the Big Hidatsa village. It has a delicate encompassable scale and the gentle deer-pressed lodge sites have a wind-soft intimacy. Bullberries grow in a rough hedge along the old fortification ditch around the landward side of the village; they are full ripe, and the chokecherries are also ready, heavy on the boughs. A family of marsh hawks wheels high overhead, crying in unison.

These village sites provide a fastening, a simple evidence of daily life in the Missouri valley that is refreshing after long contemplation of the dizzying mythic, its wheeling suns and moons. But of course even the daily details, the *culture*, shook down (and were accounted for in sophisticated ways) from the legendary foundations. Among the cast of primeval Hidatsa heroes were twin brothers who became known as "Two Men." On an expedition east of the Missouri, one of the pair ate the flesh of a gigantic two-headed snake and was immediately transformed into one himself. His brother promptly threw him over his shoulder and carried him to the Missouri and eased him into the water. His body stretched from the mouth of the Heart north to Thunder Creek ("a few miles below Sanish, North Dakota"), with a head at each end. This, needless to say, fortified Hidatsa claims to and spiritual interaction with this core-stretch of the Missouri. Grandfather Snake, as the creature came to be known, also helped the Hidatsa to cross the Missouri (taught them to build bullboats of hide and willow frames) and instructed them in other major water-related strategies.

But what I ponder here at the little everyday village on Knife River are the smaller things, the cultural traits that filtered down from the Big River and its Big Snake to places like this. Brilliant of course, Grandfather Snake sent his more mundane instructions up the tributaries, usually in the charge of a water creature like the mink or the turtle or the frog. There, up some lesser stream, these adjutant creatures spread their lore for successful agriculture, for good hunting, for healing the sick. The mink, for one, setting up along a feeder stream, taught the people that "earth, wood, stone, and water go together": hence the sweat lodge was born. The structure and tenets of the sweat lodge would lead directly to the structure and techniques for the earthlodge. From a bird's eye view of the upper Missouri, the teachings of the culture heroes flow up each tributary and into the smallest Hidatsa stream, edifying, clearing the way for human life.

From the Knife River village traces it is a short twenty-mile drive to Washburn, North Dakota, a town of 2,000 souls on the north bank of the Missouri. Washburn is the sort of going-about-its-business town that I think, for fifteen or twenty seconds, I could move to and write poems deep within a bushy-lawned old house. In another realm, it is a village set nonchalantly on the solfatara of a titanic past.

The Hidatsa accounts transcribed early this century are full of references to the town and its environs. The landing point of Charred Body—a proto-Hidatsa who descended from the sky in the form of an arrow to investigate the buffalo (he had heard them bellowing far below)—is set on Turtle Creek just outside Washburn. Charred Body soon brought down thirteen couples from the sky villages to settle the earth; Awatixa informants said their thirteen original houses were built on the banks of Turtle Creek. Most of the pantheon of demonic monsters engaged by Hidatsa culture heroes are said to have resided and prowled "just a couple of miles east of Washburn." Turtle Creek (at one time known as Charred Body Creek) hits the Missouri just below Washburn. It was—know it or not—the scene of grand and gruesome theater.

I drive south from town on Highway 83, paralleling the Missouri, until I see the creek cutting in from the east. I cross it slowly—it is a muddy, carpy little run—then turn around and drive back to the north bank and park. Between the highway and the Missouri there runs an elevated railroad right-of-way. I climb to the tracks and walk down to the old trestle bridge crossing Turtle Creek and get comfortable on a tie.

To the east I can see the creek ambling down a broad, rolling valley—her course is sketchily marked by willows. A red barn stands a mile upstream. Then, not far off, she drops slightly, squeezes ignominiously through a concrete culvert beneath U.S. 83, and enters the Missouri bottoms.

When Charred Body established the thirteen original Hidatsa settlements in these parts, the sky-colonists were not received with open arms. The evil spirit-figures residing in the neighborhood attacked them with malicious and magical force. One resident monster called Man-with-No-Head visited Charred Body's pregnant sister and ripped out her fetal twin boys. That was a mistake for the earth-ogres. Within weeks the twins grew to be powerful and fearless warriors who relentlessly sought out the enemies of the Hidatsa colonists and destroyed them one by one—a roaring giant known as Fire Moccasins (they managed to set him ablaze with his own footwear); a voracious old hag with a taste for Hidatsa flesh and a basket with powers to suck in her fleeing victims; old No-Head, with an equally insatiable cannibalistic maw located like an exposed gizzard on his trunk between his shoulders. The lads slew them all in dextrous and clever, sometimes operatic, combat, right here on Turtle Creek.

There is nothing to be done except smoke a cigarette and gaze upvalley for a quarter hour. In 1908 Edward Curtis photographed several of the mythic sites nearby (a certain tree under which Fire Moccasins is said to have habitually lounged; a pond where one of the water monsters swam). Ethnologist Martha Beckwith wrote in 1929 that remains of the original thirteen villages were "still visible." But by now I suppose those dubious points of reference are thoroughly lost and forgotten. I have created an odd silence on the trestle bridge, conjuring the sky-shuttlings and cosmological sumo battles. But then, down along the creek, bluejays take charge, stir things up in the box elders, crying "*Thief! Thief!*"

I find a pleasant, threadworn set of tourist cabins on the south side of Washburn, with roses and hollyhocks at the stoops. It is only midafternoon but I rent one from an intimidated white-haired lady peering through a small sliding cash-wicket and spend an hour lying on the spineless bed listening to the Bach partitas. I am tired of the invisible. I think of a friend standing full-face in the pure and simple specious present of the Greek surf, and then go downtown for supper.

There is a small municipal museum on the main street. I duck in for a quick look—there might be a stone hammer once used by Charred Body. When the girl at the desk asks casually what brought me to Washburn, and I allude to the monumental goings-on at Turtle Creek, she appears to be genuinely speechless for a moment. Her mouth hangs open. "At *Washburn?*"

Within minutes we are conversing softly, knowingly, sharing the intimacy of being in on a great exclusive secret. Then I cross the street to the Jewel Cafe and, happily, find a North Dakota immigrant specialty, a formidable pile of bacon, potatoes, and sauerkraut, now, having lain long together, called Knoephla.

$\sim$

Of late I have come to look on my library of plains tales—Hidatsa, Blackfoot, Crow, and all the rest—with the sort of fondness I used to carry for the Elizabethans or Balzac. They comprise, I see now (all the moreso while driving North Dakota), a Golden Age of literature for these bluffs and valleys, a Golden Age of endlessly rich and baffling Rabelaisian adventures in an unfettered, prepuritan world both light-footed and deadly. I love the stories aimless and purpose-bent as tumbleweeds, full of gravity-defiance and off-hand demolition. Stories with personages the likes of Chicken-Can't-Swim and Cedar Between the Eyes. Guts, Kidney, and Horn. One called Breathing.

$\sim$

I have saved my visit to the Singer Butte for last because its story is bright in the mythic weave. One of the heights within the Killdeer Mountains some eighty miles west from Washburn, Singer Butte represents the blending of a beautiful instinctual psychology of landscape with the transformational conviction of ritual song.

The leader of all the various butte-spirits across Hidatsa lands was a large owl who resided in the Killdeer Mountains. As each spirit—bird or animal—guarded and sustained the particular powers lodged in their butte-home, so the owl was coordinator and maestro of the entire landscape. "In the beginning," it is said, "all the gods would meet on top of the Killdeer Mountains to sing." To sing, perform their rites, to lay the very names to the land features—and give them sustaining tempo. Periodically ever since, the spirits reconvene here in concert under the owl's auspices to re-sing it all, to freshen the names of the homelands.

The Killdeers comprise a sizable rumpled uplift of heavily wooded, sparsely settled mountains. Once up among them via the jagged dirt roads there is again that northern bouquet of wet alder, willow and birch, a cool succulence after the hot plains day. I finally choose a distinguished looking bald knob, something open enough to look off from, park along the ditch, and climb off up its grassy flank.

In ten minutes I am there. It is a worthy height, commanding a view over the Killdeers and well beyond. The flatlands below are winkled by fast-moving cloud rafts. The top of the knob is wind-honed, tundra-like, with no vegetation taller than dwarfish cinquefoil. A nighthawk flushes sleepily from her nest on cool bare gravel. Scattered about are huge rock chunks, fractured plinths covered with orange lichen. They lie strewn casually about like the trampled remains of a great campfire. I get in behind one to escape the gusty west wind that is tossing the lower hardwood hills through all the facets of green.

This was the rallying point, the binder. This is the place for the singing, for the continuous *singing-through, singing-off* the layers of the pre-human, all the layers of the implacable heartless. There is an exposed beauty and vulnerability up here that fits in with the stories of supplication and insistent hymn.

In the Hidatsa creation story, Lone Man and First Creator, during their introductory chat, spoke of genealogies, charted their lonely pedigrees against the stark muck of the unformed world. Lone Man looked about him in the vast solitude (I see him idly stroking his dusty chin) and speculated. Because, while retracing his own backtrail one day not long before, he noticed flecks of blood on a tuft of wheatgrass, he inferred that that grass species was his mother. And shortly thereafter, wandering the chaos nearby, he discovered the tracks of a "stone buffalo" (a wingless brown grasshopper)—near enough his bunchgrass place-of-birth that he deduced the grasshopper was his sire.

The ancient visual base of that humble story—grasshopper adoze on hot summer wheatgrass head, nodding all day in a kind of oblivious semisexual union or samadhi—and Lone Man's nimble heroic leap connecting to the nonhuman, the wonderful child-trope of it: It is as poignant as Sophocles or *Madame Butterfly*. I will think of it all the way home as the buttes flow by.

The Heart River heart-of-the-world was difficult, tough to conjure, although now, a week later, I remember it more gently, see the fleet of geese as the key. Dog Den was wild, almost radioactively evocative. Turtle Creek was distant yet humbling; fainter than Lodi. But these Singing Hills hold a present-tense, wind-whipped, positive power. As the earlier sites and their stories elucidated the political and the cultural, the Killdeers anchor the poetical: Let it be known. "The spirits will teach you the songs and tell you the names of these high hills—There will be a great deal of memorizing."

This is the nighthawk place. The sun/shade dapple on the plains below resembles the variegated flickering of a stoney beach-bottom seen through shallow dancing water. It is simply the inkling that Song and Name, the lingual coordinates, safekeep and seal the entire earthly entourage. And it is here as of this high noon, a sense of fluent sun-lit place and rightful human hilum, sweet as cherries.

A Day
Through the Bearpaws

THE BEARPAW MOUNTAINS had acquired over the years a quintessential horizon status, a type-casting the result of seeing them so often, from so many directions, always on the far skyline, a variable archipelago pivotal to north-central Montana. Driving east or west on the Highline, U.S. 2, or pulling out from Fort Benton, or coming up from Lewistown toward the Missouri breaks, they are there sooner or later as a kind of authorization of your chosen favorite latitude.

But yesterday, I went in. I filled the water jugs in the town of Chinook and took most of the day to drive south through them. The approach from the north climbs the impeccable plano up from the Milk River valley. The ascent is slow and steady as the horizon-configuration—the low-slung off-center range—broadens and opens and eventually takes you in.

The Bearpaws consist of an extensive (some fifty miles long) system of knobs and knolls, bulges and pyramidal peaks of great variety. Despite occasional rough stone outcroppings and rugged razorbacks, the eastern Bearpaws are to a great extent grassy mountains, and, because of that, ambivalent mountains suggesting both the rugged and the cushioned. Many of the mountain-hills are entirely "bald" with grasses. Others have stands of dark pine on their upper reaches. Their ridges rise with the muscular ripple of a bull's shoulder. And below them all run sweet narrow streams through narrow meadows bearing willow heads and sunflowers and browsing pronghorns.

There is a stillness and an unoccupied, almost abandoned feel to the inner Bearpaws. (I wrote in my notebook yesterday, "One of the most isolate places ..." and then remembering so many other Montana drives, crossed it out at once.) There are a number of old cabins and ruined homesteads along the road, to be sure. But plenty of ranches still work the mountains, and to a passerby they look like some of the most prepossessing domiciles on earth. One of the distinctive features of the range is that the land is mostly privately owned. Excepting the western, skiable part of the range, over on the Rocky Boy Reservation, there is little chance for extended physical contact beyond the dirt roads and their between-fences margins.

But the visuals are top-notch. The view of the Snake Creek valley from the hill just north of Lloyd provides a spectacular example of colossal grassland uplift. Lloyd itself, or perhaps I should say "inner Lloyd," in its handsome setting, consists of a white church, a house/ parttime store hybrid, a couple of worn, all-purpose outbuildings, and several dozen Vesper sparrows. Even Cleveland, the other municipality on the maps of the eastern Bearpaws, had a working bar I remember from my only other flirtation with the area, when I drove in from the Fort Belknap Indian Days celebration for a quick look at the lovely People's Creek country, turned around in Cleveland, and drove back to the powwow.

The hills, the hill-mountains below Lloyd, have the delicate edgework of the northern latitudes, poised on the verge of the northland as they are. On the north-facing grassy slopes tight little choirs of popple stand, shivering and eager. Good places to crawl in and sleep, I say. But then, I have an inherited instinct I refer to as the "hollow log syndrome." It is a documented part of my patrimony and involves a rather continual taking note of promising places to curl up out of the weather and sleep in private, beyond-the-pale anonymity: a hollow log in a snowstorm; a protective limestone ledge; abandoned bridge abutments; a vegetated crease in a hillside. Those inviting popple stands reminded me of it, as did a neat and out-of-the-way yard of big jellyroll haybales farther down the road. A curious blend of vestigial canniness and schoolboy fantasia, it is like thin woodsmoke above a departed Jungian camp. I have put it to good use on occasion when hitchhiking cross-country, and I wonder some days just how many generations it goes back.

Historians write that the range was named in the 1850s by a survey party that claimed, viewing the mountains from a high point to the southwest, they resembled a grizzly track; the original version was "Bear's Paw." And that during the 1920s' drought and depression, the region's homesteaders were devastated, the streams and coulees of the inner range filled with scanty desperate shacks and shanties.

The road is a pleasure to know. Like the hills, it is varied, pastoral, quiet as a cave. I hadn't seen a vehicle since I topped that hill north of Lloyd and noticed a small dustcloud to the east—someone buzzing into Chinook for groceries.

Most of the cattle grazing contentedly on the high knob-tops are the hardy Angus breed, familiar with the boreal. Sixteen or eighteen miles south of Lloyd I stop to walk the road a while. It was probably the upper Cow Creek valley, I decided today while studying the atlas. It was an open, mixed-grass area with the Little Rockies hanging on the horizon to the east. There was just enough wind in the place I decided to walk the roadside prairie and practice my longspurring. Longspurring is a little-known sport endemic to the high plains grasslands. It is not simply watching for and observing longspurs and other prairie passerines in their habitat. Longspurring involves the studied use of wind to provide better-than-average views of the birds. The technique can salvage a certain type of May or June day when the wind is running high enough to discourage most pastimes, even hike-dawdling. You proceed to a sizable tract of shortgrass land and quarter into the wind, watching for small birds flushing. When they go up, the wind will usually (a) slow their departure, and (b) shorten their flight by 90 percent. Their instinct is to flush away from your approach, thus into the wind, which slaps them down quickly. The wind-hampered rise allows the longspurrer to follow the bird in the binoculars and watch it set down not-so-far-off, providing a good clear view of the specimen, as opposed to the normal evanescent glimpse. It is a sport no more dubious than, say, curling. ... I had little luck in the Bearpaws. Maybe the longspurs have already drifted south, or maybe, even though these mountains are grassy mountains, there is too much uplift for their taste. I jumped only a few Lark sparrows, and a handful of prairie Chippies.

Twenty minutes later I was out of the Bearpaws and onto the high, unsociable sage plain between the range and the Missouri River, driving a disinterested time-free dirt road leading to the breaks. I played again a remarkable tape I had listened to the preceding several days, a tape of Lakota scalp songs originally composed and sung in the immediate aftermath of the Little Bighorn fight. The songs were recorded not long ago, to the accompaniment of a hand drum, by Wilmer Mesteth, an Oglala man of the Pine Ridge Reservation, who learned the songs from family elders and other tribal members who had preserved the songs from previous generations. Fourteen songs in all, unified as they are by a common subject, the collection has an almost eerie sense of historical freshness-at-hand, in addition to the palpable pleasure of the sudden reconstitution of such history-specific documents that might have been lost forever.

There is a song honoring Sitting Bull, and the very song that Crazy Horse's mother sang after he was killed at Fort Robinson in Nebraska, a lovely, elegiac song: "When you see the Black Hills remember me ..." Several of the celebratory post-battle songs are enough to provoke gooseflesh. Comprised of two or three oft-repeated lines, they sing, "The Long Knives made a great charge—Now they are crying," and "The soldiers made us angry—Now we have their flag," and "I warned Custer not to come, warned his scouts—They must not have told him," and "Thank you, Long Knives, for all the guns you brought." But the brief, respectfully tempoed one called "Custer's Wife" is wonderful.

A Day Through the Bearpaws

Custer's wife is still waiting,
worrying. She is crying, keeps looking
up this way.

Yow.

Finally the junipers appear, a smattering at first, then
pines, and I drop the great and tortuous drop into the
Missouri breaks and onto the narrow bench of the big
river. It has been, roughly, an eighty-mile day, seven
hours' worth, from the Milk to the Missouri. I drive
upstream about a mile along the sage-flat north bank,
and then there is the lone trailer in sight, and the Mc-
Clelland ferry rig, and a dark dog napping in the sun.

The ferryman had seen me coming and was already
putting across the stream to fetch me. The river wasn't
more than thirty yards wide. The ferryman was quite
deaf and very self-conscious of that fact; he tended to
smother the issue by avoiding conversation, but at last,
as we stood at the ferry rail on the south bank I got him
going a little. Some days he sees only a single car, or
two. Some days a dozen. He is about sixty-five and a
native of this specific stretch of river.

He began to reminisce about the large cottonwood
groves that stood along its banks fifty years ago. The
huge ice buildup of 1947 sliced them clean off, and no
trees to speak of have gotten a foothold since. There
was one in particular, "the Big Tree" he calls it, that

stood off on the grassy bench just east of the trailer. It had a large iron ring circling it, which his father figured dated from the 1870s when it served as a tie-up for the Fort Benton-bound steamboats. The ice of '47 got that tree, too. He remembered once when he was a boy, they were shearing sheep nearby, and the Big Tree threw shade enough to cool a flock of 500 head.

Then he was tired of talking. A bit rusty, I presume. I got in my car and drove down the ramp. An isolate man in an isolate place. But all the same, on second thought that word is not the right one yet again. He is in fact knotted comfortably into a civil and affectionate nexus, Missouri breaks style: He keeps three trotlines in the river almost continually when the water is fishable. He told me yesterday he had three nice catfish tethered on a stringer at the moment. "One for a friend of mine down the road. And I'll give one to another fellow who ranches up on the tableland. He likes catfish. And I'll keep one for myself."

On Cherry Creek

YESTERDAY I STOPPED to dig prairie turnips in southeastern Montana. It was public land on the high divide between the Tongue and Powder rivers: that heady stratum of open pine-wooded mountain knolls in June with the sweet clover and Mariposa lilies blooming and the dense indigo blossom of the psoralea turnip—*tinpsila,* the Sioux word, is better. I spent two hours there digging them up with the large blade of my pocket knife for lack of a stronger tool.

It took me twenty minutes to unearth an average plant, a tuber about two and a half inches long and an inch in diameter, by digging down along the thin subterranean stem to reach the widening root at a depth of three or four inches, then carefully scraping away the dirt around it until it could be pulled free unbroken. The procedure left a fist-wide, wrist-deep hole and blisters on the knuckles. It is the sort of lost-in-task work that inevitably engages the nonhuman. I looked up now and then to find Lark sparrows and jays, and once a Mountain bluebird, sitting nearby, watching with considerable interest.

It also attracted a tall, pale, near-albino man with a parsnip-colored beard. He was camping in a pine grove a hundred yards away and walked over to ask if I had any extra drinking water. He had the distinct aura about him of tottering on the very verge of losing the basic social fluency of his species. He had long fluted fingernails and a thin layer of soilage. He stood watching me dig, laughing a dry marsupial laugh. He asked if I would take him into Miles City to get supplies; I explained I was traveling the opposite direction.

But other than those five minutes I was alone with the tinpsila digging and lost in the root-digger's timeless back-aching mentality: On all fours amid the June grass and salsify and sunny blue flax, peering into a hand-sized hole while the Upland sandpipers whistled at large. I remembered the plains tribes' stories of women—sky-dwelling myth women—pulling up turnips and peeking into such a divot to discover a whole new world in there, sighting new blue sky with white clouds and something like the Earth and all its alluring wonders spread far below.

To glimpse the mythic it helps if you put yourself in a mythic position. Sometime while scraping away at the third tinpsila I realized the sandpipers' wolfish whistles might well be directed at me in my vulnerable all-fours posture. And then I digressed good naturedly into a turnip fantasy of getting my fist stuck in the hole and starving there, good naturedly, eventually drying up and blowing away after breaking off at the wrist the very way tinpsila plants break off and disappear after flowering (so that they won't all be found and extinguished at once).

After two hours I had half a dozen goodsized roots, plus a runt, a dud. I peeled the dark brown skin off the latter and ate it. But I was saving the others especially for today.

This morning I drove out from Faith, South Dakota, south for a few miles and then off to the southeast on the unpaved Red Scaffold road. I was going to Cherry Creek. I am always happy when I'm going to Cherry Creek, happy as breakfast, for no other reason than the joy of her rivers and hills. And to drive there on the Red Scaffold road is to get it at its best, to approach a magnanimous place through a progression of unadulterated topological elegance that nearly amounts to a protocol.

First there is Red Scaffold Creek off to the left, a small stream cutting a steep wooded course, and soon there is Cherry Creek to the right, her deep dense valley moving below bold grassland hills. This part of the Cheyenne River drainage is probably the loftiest, purest, most uninterrupted land I know in the west. The little road rides it, tacks with the steady patient narrowing of the uplands, then drops neatly to the confluence of the two streams, where the hamlet of Red Scaffold convenes.

And now we are with Cherry Creek herself for fifteen miles of sinuous descent no thing short of deluge can hurry. Native grasses and yellow sweet clover color the strong upper hills, hills enough to send one back to Faith to leave a scrap of highgrade offering at the highway corner shrine to Our Lady of Beauraing. Gradually, the valley widens, the cottonwoods grow more matronly. Ten miles below Red Scaffold another perfect little stream makes an entrance, minnows in from the north.

Closer to the mouth of Cherry Creek, the ultimate confluence of the day, where it joins the full-grown Cheyenne River, occasional cedars scatter on the booming hills. An occasional house; horses bunched in windy sun. There is a beautiful outhouse toilet set on one of the ridges, set aptly with its doorless door overlooking the wide valley. Then, after an hour of it, with a final swirl and turn we drop over a hill and into the village of Cherry Creek, aflutter with much wash on the lines. Spring or Fall, there is always a grand sense of arrival.

South Dakota maps give its population as 300. The houses—eighty or a hundred of them, some of them crumbling turn-of-the-century reservation stucco, some in tracts just a few years old—are situated on the northeast side of the Cherry Creek–Cheyenne River intersection in an accommodating basin. The hills go up on three sides. There is a small white-washed pow-wow arbor adjacent to a dusty rodeo ground and ball-field whose dugouts are roofed with pine boughs. There are three churches, and a horse herd at the west edge of town.

One modest commercial building houses a part-time post office and a one-time general store with gas pumps in front. On a slope at the northeast edge of town is a long-standing, long-leaking communal well, whose water, most residents agree, is suspect. But if you time it right you can buy cold pop from a private home with an extra refrigerator on the west side, in the newer part of town toward the creek.

Cherry Creek is some thirty-five miles from towns of any size, including Eagle Butte, the reservation capital, and fifteen or twenty miles from the state highways to the east and west, the nearest bridges. It is obvious after a few moments in the sun and the silence even teenagers can't break that human beings have sought out and lived in this good place for a long, long time.

The Cheyennes were here early on. Lewis and Clark reported that tribe "living principally along this river" that had already taken their name. A General Atkinson wrote in 1826 that the Cheyennes' "trading ground is at the mouth of Cherry River, a branch of the Chey-enne." And people were no doubt here generations be-fore those notations, and generations before that peo-

ples now known by little save the cut of their projec-
tiles points were coming up the Cheyenne River from
the great Missouri (fifty miles east) to settle in this
place. Good wood, good water, good buffering hills.

And after the Cheyennes migrated west the Sioux
peoples found the place—forebears of the present Min-
niconjou community, including the band of Big Foot
that in December 1890 left this very site, harried and
confused, and ended up a week later on a creek named
Wounded Knee.

It is admiration for this almost tangible sense of orig-
inal-population-in-place, this layering, together with
the unpresuming harmonics stubborn in the isolate lay
of the place, that brings me here at some point every
year. Whatever the season, I always end up doing the
same things. After the lazy approach and a slow loop
through town I stop at the post office and let someone
know I'd like to climb the big hill south of town. I park
off the road just west of the Cherry Creek bridge and
angle up the slope. In half an hour I am atop the formidable rise and looking off a long way.

The Cheyenne River forks at a remote and cotton-
wood-heavy point some fifty miles west of here. Both
forks rise in the northeast quadrant of Wyoming; more
significantly, as a pair of conceptual "tongs" they en-
close, or cup, the Black Hills in a pregnant, beneficent

design. That is certainly part of the river's legendary goodness.

Twenty miles west of here the Highway 73 bridge spans her at a handsome point. It is a modern bridge across a valley almost a mile in width. Like all bridges it is a lightning rod and focal point for river things. There is usually something of interest going on there or something just-done. It's a quiet spot, save for the occasional unpredictable *bong* of the bridge metal and the numerous Cliff swallows calling—a sizable colony nests under the bridge. They buzz me annually, swirling and holding close overhead, craning for a good clear look. The intricate car-struck dead ones lay tossed and desiccating like flies in an attic window.

The river marks the southern border of the Cheyenne River Sioux Reservation. There are always beer cans under the bridge and a splash of fierce graffiti, and bare footprints in the mud of both shores, with heron tracks mixed in. One day while loitering on the span I met a Lakota man walking across the bridge alone with a light jacket over his shoulder. I had seen him coming down the long slope to the north. We had a nice talk. He was walking to Rapid City, some 120 miles west of here—but of course he would get a lift before long, we all knew that.

Another time there was a tony white man down on the south bank just off the bridge, watering down a matching trio of brindle boxers on a long trident leash, and once an old Sioux man gazing through binoculars on the north side who wouldn't acknowledge my presence for anything I hollered or waved. One morning I stood mid-bridge in a mild seethe considering a passage I had read the night before in John Moore's *The Cheyenne Nation,* in which the author has the cloistered theory-coddled gall to quote Josef "The Boot" Stalin in a scholarly context callously directed at those oft-brutalized people; a kingfisher finally broke it.

On another visit there was nothing but a coyote pup run over on the bridge—certainly not long before I got there—plump and pretty, with a little smile on its face. Just a tyke—never even got to know the taste of mutton. ...

Here at Cherry Creek the Cheyenne swings parabolically through its wide bottoms, a boulevard if ever there was one. Beyond the river on nonreservation land stand the prudent stacks of a large hay operation, just visible through the cottonwood groves. There is the perpetual breeze bouncing the upland grasses. A dog barks in the town below. Children on bikes; white crosses gleaming in the four cemeteries.

And today I have tinpsila. This is precisely the place I wanted to eat them: a long-frequented place; a place named, as an extra measure, after primary food. Chokecherries are heavy on their bushes in creases of the upper hills. A few plums are coming on in the lower patches, hard and green as new olives.

I also have cheddar and saltines. The latter are light enough to require battening against the wind. When I peel the skin from a turnip there is a lustrous flash of clean white subterranean flesh. Raw, they taste something like uncooked green peas fresh from the pod. They have the texture of raw cashews.

They are the gatherers' June food. By the end of the month the upper plant will have disappeared until next spring. A friend down near Oglala told me that when he was a boy (this was probably in the 1920s) his entire family would load a wagon with cooking and sleeping gear come mid-June and set out after tinpsila. They traveled the piney hill country for ten days or more, slow and easy, digging the roots all day and braiding them into long bunches for drying. It was total and gregarious immersion in the first wave of summer largesse.

A month later it will be the namesake cherries, red as chert, black as coal, and later yet the wild plums, in late September, their good-crop years inciting a simple hand-to-mouth elation of succulence-for-the-taking like no other—except maybe the black currants in their late-summer prime.

Chokecherries are certainly the archetypal given-food by virtue of their arm's reach abundance and reliability. They are not temperamental like the plums; they will pretty much be there in July and on through the summer, a heavy and crow-black load on the bushes open to all mouths. In good years it is a load unto listless glut that dizzies the dickey birds and sickens the 'coons. They hang, festoon, as the image of Plenty-for-a-change and a fanfare for the cornucopia.

A few years ago just north of Lame Deer, Montana, I saw a man seated on top of a stepladder in a mature cherry patch, picking contentedly with both hands. One August along a small creek in Colorado I came across two men, self-taught vintners, hard at work in a cherry stand, filling large cardboard boxes with fruit. They were red-faced and happy. I suspect they had just finished off the final bottle of last year's vintage over lunch.

I remember walking railroad tracks along the Bad River with a friend during a summer when the cherries were so abundant and water-fat the bushes strained with their weight, shaking and bursting with songbirds; the squirrels and wild turkey flocks were red-around-the-mouth and saucer-eyed with gorging on them. And that same month, groups of children at a small rural powwow on the Pine Ridge Reservation wandering about with fruit-laden cherry branches in hand, eating them like cotton candy.

In comparison, this tinpsila is quiet, bread-like, a simple staple. During the old days here the pulverized dried roots—"tinpsila flour"—was a favored trade good. In a classic tame-for-wild exchange, the horticultural tribes of the upper Missouri villages gave three measures of corn for one of prairie turnip flour to thicken their gruels.

Those Cherry Creek trade fairs were famous on the northern plains. It was a site of high commerce and exotic barter. Grizzly bear teeth, obsidian, dentalium shells, meadowlark and cardinal skins. Brain-tanned buckskin, elk tushes, woodpecker scalps. Turmeric to dye porcupine quills—the aesthetic necessities. As well as salt, pipestone, mica. Magpie feathers and gunpowder. Unborn antelope hides. I think of all that coming and going as I look down on the roads today, the lovely elemental roads in and out, gravel-slow, upriver, downriver, upcreek, off into the folds of the hills north. "They all lead to Cherry Creek."

So this morning I came to sit and look again at these hills to reaffirm a sense of Place-as-fruit, with fresh tinpsila on the side. No other place has quite the same feel of grass and earth and water configured just right, and I come back to commit it to memory for a while. The high hills holding their multilingual dead. The centuries of deals well-done. ... Meadowlark skins—I must have passed three dozen dead meadowlarks on the highway the past few days.

A gunshot thuds from one of the cottonwood groves down the Cheyenne bottoms, thuds through the deep silence cottoned by wind. Down below, a car is creeping along through the grassy plaza around the Cherry

Creek powwow arbor. It drives slowly around the edge of the field. Stops on the near side. Backs up. Goes on around, and jockeys back a second time. Whoever is in there obviously sees me—and is wondering. It might well be the same man who accosted me suspiciously last year while I was writing in my notebook over by the community pump, came to see who I was and what I was doing, so far from highway. And now he's spotted me again. It's time to leave. Time to get up, go back where I came from.

History & Then Some

ROBERT HUMMINGBIRD was a Kiowa man who had moved north a long time ago. His southern name still stood out among the Charging Eagles, Red Bulls, and Thunder Hawks of North and South Dakota. Robert operated a small gas station and store at the junction of Hominy and Hickory creeks along a lonesome edge of the big reservation. He was a stout, photogenic man who from the looks of him should have been a cowhand or a telephone lineman or a government hunter, but he ran the little store at the forks. The streams themselves were muddy, spindly runs, insignificant one would assume; yet alive enough that you heard now and then at the coffee counter or around the gas pumps references to "Hominy people" and "Hickory people," clans living on the respective banks up in the dry piney hills, lineages that, one soon inferred, lit their fires from radically different coals.

Robert always had a good story cached somewhere near at hand. I usually took him a sack of oranges and he told me a story. He told his tales well; knew what people liked and how to please them and tweak their ear. Old stories and new, happy, sad, funny. He knew just when and where to call them in.

One afternoon I stopped to see him and we decided to take a short walk, the day was so inviting—a sunny, dancing day with a jig of a wind in the trees. Outside the store, Robert looked around: "Hickory or Hominy?" We crossed the road and started up the slope along Hickory Creek. A runt blue roan of a dog hobbled after us. Robert said, "Let's go up to those pretty plum trees," nodding at a red-orange thicket up the hill. When we reached the plums we stopped, looked back over the September valley. The two halting little streams, Hominy and Hickory, working down from their hills, each had a few box elders in bright color. Just a stone's throw from Robert's store the two broke character, jumped realm, reluctantly merged to become Hagerty Draw.

"This place doesn't smell too good," Robert said. "Must be a dead skunk in those bushes." He pointed across the hillside and we walked over there to a patch of yellow milkweeds and sat down among them. Robert was in a quiet mood, but slowly rallied.

"I know you like history," he said after a few minutes.

"I try to like it."

"I can tell you like it."

Then he told me a brief tale, with history in it.

Just after the Korean War, when a lot of Indian soldiers came back with combat stories and medals and
there were honoring songs and dances every week,
some of the young boys got excited by all the valorous
talk. There were two boys, cousins of Robert's wife,
who decided to find some adventure of their own.
They were Robert's pals, just a few years younger than
he was. Smart boys, about eighteen years of age, and
they had good senses of humor. Because they had
missed the big war, they decided they would go down,
just the two of them, to Oklahoma and pull a raid on
their traditional enemies of yore, the Pawnees.

So in the springtime they took a bus all the way
from Bismarck to Stillwater, Oklahoma. From there
they hitchhiked on over to the town of Pawnee. They
slept in the woods that night and early the next morning they found a car on a side street of Pawnee and got
in it and drove away. "I don't know if they hot-wired
it or if they found the keys in it. I can't remember anymore."

They didn't mean any harm. They thought it was a
great lark. They just drove off at first light and took the
car back over to the outskirts of Stillwater, not too far
away. Then they parked it and found an Indian boy
walking to school and had him take a picture of them
in front of the car with their Brownie camera before
they went back to the bus station and came home. That

was the last raid on the Pawnees. Those boys told that story a hundred times the rest of their lives.

"We had that picture around for a long time. I don't know what happened to it. Arella doesn't take care of things like she should."

After a while we got up and walked on across the hillside to Hominy Creek and followed it down toward the store, not saying much. We were down on the lower meadow, walking past a marshy cattail place in the creek when we heard something splashing about in the willows, then someone talking gruffly. Then we could see him: a wiry little man, lurking, cringing, glaring at us, holding onto a willow tree. He was streaming wet and unshaven. I thought he looked like William Tecumseh Sherman run amok. He was raving in a sputtering gutteral mutter, something about "Bloodsuckers," something about "Sidemeat."

Robert and I had both stopped in our tracks. "Just look right at him," Robert told me. "Look him right in the eye." And the steady gaze from the two of us quieted the man. He quit ranting, and a few seconds later slinked back into the cattails and out of sight.

"His name is Schlegel," Robert said as we moved on. "They're Germans. Hominy people. They've ranched over in there about a hundred years."

The following spring I passed through again—"beach-combing," as Robert's wife called it, she had a talented mean streak—and stopped at the store for coffee. Robert asked me if I remembered the old coot preaching sidemeat in the willows. He informed me that Schlegel had died during the winter. Had driven himself fifteen miles into the county seat one day and lain down spreadeagle on the courthouse lawn and died. Robert was surprised I hadn't read about it in the Denver papers; it was big news in those parts. They did an autopsy on the man. Word got out pretty soon they found a thatch of thick red hair growing all over his heart.

Grand River, Again

THIS MORNING I am going out to see the South Fork of Grand River in Perkins County, South Dakota, upstream from the Shadehill Dam. Yesterday, when I drove up into this corner of the state, was ennervatingly hot, but a boomer of an electrified cold front passed through last night and civilized things quickly, made the entire mission seem well-timed and cogent.

I walk or loiter along rivers like this one so often, rally the same or similar thoughts and eyesful that I begin to feel, this morning at any rate and for the very first time, like John Donne with his Sermons. Each time I come to the Grand River National Grasslands (once every four or five years is not enough) is, admittedly, devotional and tonic and I inevitably fill pages of my pocket notebook and end up a few weeks after with a poem or a sketch, or even a would-be Sermon, a soliloquy on a Point Perceived as Relevant to the Soule and Passed Along. And the Subject is always the sense of rivers and their uplands as sensual mentalities, as organisms subtle and fine, to be encountered like music or cool baywater.

But for one reason or another I have never devoted ample time to the South Fork of the Grand, and here I am today with that in mind and oranges in my pack and a grasslands map to pick out the public from the private lands. I select a stretch sixteen or eighteen miles southwest of the Shadehill lake and climb the fence.

Were I a landscape painter I would spend a lot of time in the Grand River country. It is a grassland landscape of endless richness and chromatic mood, elegant as the oftpainted Marin hills of California. Today, in early August, the first of the grasses are beginning to color, break toward Fall, and the scattered chapparal-like patches of chokecherry and bullberry have a slightly changed cast to them on the far hills' runnels below an expansive crennelated skyline. Like all the Grand River terrain, it has a welling, formidable noblesse.

I walk west on the high bench for half a mile, then cut south toward the stream. Upland sandpipers flush off right and left. It is so windy this morning I have to wear sunglasses and keep my lips firmly closed to avoid the endless spray of large grasshoppers that, in a 25 or 30 mph wind, slap hard into the face and would no doubt lodge deep in an unguarded gullet. So windy that I have to kneel and take hold of the bouncing grasses to distinguish various specimens. In ten minutes I top the fifty-foot bluffs on the north side of the river. It is a wide, unoccupied bottom here, perhaps a mile across at this point between major bends, soft and green with this year's wet summer. It is classic Bovinia; there are cattle on the distant hillsides and a single ranch visible far to the south. A few minimal cottonwood groves dot the valley. We are, I would guess, some one hundred miles, not counting the many kinks, from the mouth of the Grand, where it joins the Missouri near Mobridge.

I follow the bluff tops southwesterly until I strike a partly wooded draw and detour some thirty yards to investigate a dense dark ash tree at the head of the coulee. Gnarled and scarred, it is an old tree gone soft at the core; but its shade is deep Arcadian and the spinach-green of its foliage is restful on the wind-battered eye. I follow the draw, a cowpath along the draw, down toward the river, through buckbrush and scattered sagebrush. Rock wrens *tweee* and the kingbirds are very interested in my presence. It's downright hot in the valley out of the wind. As I approach the riverbank dozens of small frogs leap into the water or flee along the grassy bank—leopardy-looking fellows with a yellow stripe flowing back from each eye.

Now I am "on the water." Upstream a few hundred yards the bluffs pull back from the river and the north shore swale is easy, luxuriant walking accompanied by sweet clover and sunflowers. I stop to rest on a crumbly spit. Now even the one ranch is out of sight. The valley is busy with dragonflies. I lift the binoculars to look at one—medium-size, a boiled-cabbage green—

perched photogenically on a sunflower head ten yards off, and think instantly of W. H. Hudson praising field glasses as high among the most beneficent inventions of the modern era.

Each summer for the past few years I have spent a morning or two studying the dragonflies. It is a pastime that sneaks up on me, and it always occurs toward the end of July or the first of August on a day when the birding has slowed to a grinding halt. Then, afield and ready, I notice the dragon- and damselflies, and soon I am glassing them at the edges of streams and ponds, remarking on their aerodynamics and sheer numbers in the lower skies, even stalking them on the ratty old cattail stands. Cheyenne wisemen, after all, classified them as full-fledged birds. It is trying, tiresome work, trying to get a good look. Sometimes I take notes and look them up in the insect guide when I get home; though I can't remember ever positively identifying even one species. But it is largely an homage to the very presence of the creatures and their ethereal, omnidimensional, motordriven lives. Visually, they combine pure lapidary brilliance with the complex delicacy of the virtuoso trout fly and the sure choreography of the Japanese tea ceremony. (I have always found the fly-tiers' appellation "spent damsel" completely breathtaking.)

The longer you watch them, the more personality you can infer, which is a major breakthrough for the insect realm. In some ways they are more fascinating than birds: their effortless, fleshless flight, their acrobatic mating in midair. Their mysterious mechanics; surely their eyes must be larger than their brains. Their names are as evocative as those of birds. Bluebells and Flying Adders and Bluets. Amberwings and Saddlebags and Dancers. Hudson mentions a brilliant turquoise specimen in England they call the "Kingfisher." Dragonflies jockey and joust, chase and play like birds. They cock their heads, ponder and tally, they stretch and preen. They cast a skittery shadow. They twitch like horses. And most of all, they reconnoitre.

I've been watching a black one with a lavish-blue tail section and blue-white wings. But it is eye-tiring work keeping up with them. As an avocation, as an admittedly stop-gap avocation during the birding doldrums, seasonal as sweetcorn, dragonfly watching is a rewarding sport good for at least an hour a year, best broken into ten- or fifteen-minute terms.

Farther upstream, the river bends sharply to the south and the valley beyond is a vast expanse of unexpurgated prairie where prairiedogs yap and an eagle soars. Turning south with the stream, I find the going easier with the wind now at my back and the hoppers less threatening accordingly. I follow her till she bends westerly again at a sagebrushy, mouse-brown bluff, casts off toward the headwaters far out beyond the Slim Buttes country west of Buffalo. Then I take a long pull of water and turn back, against the wind, through the shank-high grasses rippling with it, flashing silken sheen like flame before it.

After twenty minutes I detour for a break in a handy little basin-grove beneath one huge cottonwood more than six feet through and a retinue of mature, wind-twisted willows. It is a welcome quiet place that has obviously sheltered many cattle over the years. Eventually I notice a half-grown kingbird lying dead in the patchy grass. It has a grim but somehow tolerant, clamped-matador kind of look on its face.

Then I strike off for the road and the car and the bologna sandwich. The hue of the distant bullberry patches is an argent/olive. At one point, slanting up toward the blufftops again, I thought I heard someone calling my name, several times, in a casual, friendly way from far upwind, and actually stopped and looked a time or two. That old inveterate high plains aeolian trick, always good for a laugh, eon after eon.

~

It would be nice to float the Grand all the way from the Shadehill dam to the Missouri. Factoring in the kinks and hesitations it would likely come to 200 canoe miles, most all of it through the Standing Rock Sioux Reservation, the entire first two-thirds of the trip drifting through nearly roadless, townless prairie whose hills, come sundown, seven-thirty or a quarter-of-eight, throw some of the finest shadows on earth. Past the little Hunkpapa village of Bullhead with its Doughboy statue, then the magnificent valley of Sitting Bull's camp and death site, and the vague locations of the old Ree earthlodge towns (an early native name for the Grand was "Ree River"), past Little Eagle and the larger Missouri-edge hills, around the bend and into the bay of the big river.

Later in the day I drive from my Hugh Glass Campground camp over to hike a short stretch of the North Fork. It is tougher to get at this stream than the South Fork; most of it passes through private ranchland. But I'll settle for a mile or so not far above the reservoir.

The valley here is considerably less expansive than the terrain I walked this morning. It is a tighter valley by far, with brushy hills near at hand: skunkbrush and currants and chokecherry bushes laden with tent caterpillar gauze, all charged by the perpetual Dakota wind. Yellowthroats and Song sparrows sing as the afternoon begins to weaken.

I gradually realize that I am happiest in places, I should probably say habitats, where both Eastern and Western kingbirds are present. Places like this one, and the South Fork this morning. It makes for a sort of satisfying transcontinental dovetail. I hike beside the North Fork downstream to a small point where a muddy, sedgy creek with minnows enters, and sit down among the sandreed and sunflowers. I suppose that the Hugh Glass story well deserves to be added to my hypothetical syllabus of North American readings, along beside Cabeza de Vaca and the Coyote tales, and the Lewis and Clark Journals and Ishi's story. It was in some brushy coulee near the forks of Grand River that the grizzly got him in August of 1823 and his fellow trappers left him to die and from whence he began the great mauled crawl cross-Dakota some 200 miles to Fort Kiowa on the Missouri. It was a transect on a par with Joseph and the Nez Perces. It has a multilevel moral John Donne would appreciate and the savory testimonial fierceness that comes especially from persons crawling through prickly pear for nights on end: One knows where one has been. There is a stone raised in the man's memory over on the south side of the lake.

A few of the chokecherry bushes are turning and some of the sunflowers are letting go. The second week of August. "In heaven it is alwaies Autumne," Donne says. There are so many kingbirds in this country I might have dubbed it Kingbird River if I had had a chance. I walk back toward the car through a weedy meadow that has a distinctly middlewestern look to it, and pick a handful of sage to take back to the camp and mix with the South Fork bundle I picked this morning, as the aroma-loving Symmetry Lords demand. There is a handsome orange-scarlet dragonfly zooming about among the mullein heads; I catch up with it in the glasses for a moment as it monomaniacally gauges something or other via quick six-inch forward and backward bursts. It's the color of tiger lily, Blackburnian throat. But I've had my hour of that for this summer, and the first wave of brown-eyed, warm-blooded southbound shorebirds will be showing up any day now for sure.

A River & a Range

I'M NOT MUCH of a fisherman by anybody's standards. I get out perhaps once every third year. In fact, the only waters that truly incite me to wet a line nowadays are the patient, shaded-by-sycamore smallmouth bass streams east of the Mississippi, and they do so in great part for sentimental, topopsychological reasons. But the Little Bighorn River has always been an exception. I have driven its lower course a good many years, the stretch along Highway 89 between Wyola and Hardin, Montana; have admired it early autumn mornings and watched the Crow kids splash and swim below its various bridges on hot summer days; and have often thought that fishing it, even a quick roadside stop, would be an honor.

This summer I finally set a morning aside for it, a morning of passing-through that I would lengthen by half a day and get that particular river fantasia off my mind and out of my system. The name itself, of course, and all its history is part of the attraction, and it is immediately thrown into mild controversy: The sign at Wyola pointing the way up the river's valley where it separates from the highway reads "Little Horn Road," and it is possible, I've discovered, to while away considerable time pondering the etymological nuances between the Bighorn and the Little Horn rivers as opposed to the Bighorn and its simple diminutive tributary the Little Bighorn. I finally learned from George Bird Grinnell, that conservator of countless invaluable things, that many northern plains tribes' names for the two rivers were the same: "Sheep River" and "Little Sheep River"; a diminutive of rivers, not of sheep or horns. So it seems the Little Horn is either cozy local vernacular, diminutive of a diminutive, or just a careless bastardization.

I wasn't even sure the river had fish in it. Glimpses from the road had often looked promising. But when I stopped that morning at a fishing store in Hardin to buy an embarrassingly minimal supply of Royal Wulffs and Hopper patterns (flies a friend had recommended for blind-date waters), and asked about the Little Bighorn, the help looked at me as if I were feebleminded. But it was apparent they knew nothing about the river, save that the teenage "rowdies" down around Wyola and Lodgegrass could be troublesome, even dangerous. But one hears that sort of largely benighted and superstitious hobgoblin talk from about 85 percent of white people in Indian country.

I stopped at the tribal offices in Crow Agency and eventually talked with a Fish and Wildlife man. It was a brief conversation: The Little Bighorn on the reservation was closed to all fishing. I didn't ask why, but I presume the prestigious and heavily trammeled Bighorn just to the west kept the Crow fish wardens very busy and that one corridor of intense Caucasian tourism was probably enough. But, the man finally intimated, there were private, non-Indian ranches up the Little Bighorn valley between Wyola and the Wyoming state line. Fishing on those waters was entirely up to the ranchers. "But make sure you find out the boundaries. If you get caught on tribal land you'll be arrested for trespassing."

I drove south along the river itself to Wyola and cut, at long last, up the Little Horn road. The valley was as pretty as I had imagined all those years, and grew moreso the farther southwest I drove and the closer to the Bighorn Mountains I got. After fifteen miles I noted a couple of big ranches, but continued up to a bridge near the state border. The water every place I saw it looked perfectly trouty, mountain-clear and spirited, running over fist-size boulders the color of brown-speckled hens' eggs.

I drove back to the first ranch and knocked at the door of the house. Nobody home. They were probably cutting hay somewhere down the valley. Then I drove several miles to a huge ranch set-up called the Sunlight

Ranch. From the looks of it this spread controls eight or ten miles of the finest Little Bighorn bottomlands. In a well-cared-for grove stood the original home. I walked across a large lawn and knocked. No reply. There were half a dozen other structures nearby, smaller dwellings and a fleet of work and storage buildings. I stopped at one of the houses and raised a woman who wasn't sure about fishing on the ranch. She directed me across the way to the ranch office. They would know in there for sure.

The young woman at the desk in the office spoke with the royal "we" of the landowner. She was friendly enough, but their policy in general was a No Fishing policy, like the Crows. It simplifies things, I suppose. I complimented the valley and its handsome hills and chatted for a moment. She was friendly enough, though her pencil was poised in casual midair; I thought for a second she would break, give in; I detected a surge of pure motherly, or even maidenly, sympathy. But no.

As I walked to the car the woman in the first house called from the kitchen window to learn what the boss had said. Then she turned to consult someone in the room behind her about fishing up by the stateline bridge. She thought it was public; the other thought not.

I stopped again down the road to ask a man resting at the edge of a hayfield. He was a hired man. He wasn't sure about the state-line bridge either, but he thought there was a public fishing site downvalley five miles at a small county bridge on a dirt road just off the highway. I followed his directions and twenty minutes later found the place. But the bridge and its approach were cordoned off and a sizable work crew swarmed about and huge construction machinery rattled away at the pilings.

And that was that. I'd been two and a half hours cruising the river and leaning over its bridges and stopping at ranches. And that was that, for now: sealed off, with my mouth watering at that thoroughbred stream and its valley.

It ended up becoming an exercise in disembodied Platonic mime-fishing. Not just barbless, but hookless, even rodless fishing. Not that the morning was wasted; the road was a new one for me, and those are increasingly harder to come by. And there are always the dependable intangibles to fall back on. I remembered a long, blustery autumn day last decade when I hunted sage grouse near Walden, Colorado. A long, tiring eight-hour day tromping the endless sagebrush of North Park. I'd never gone after sagehens before, and I wasn't about to give up. I saw one bird at a distance the entire outing. But that night in the motel, and next day in my car, my hunting trousers smelled so strong of sage the air was thick with it, positively heavy with it, pungent as rank hawthorn blow, and I knew suddenly that that was the residual payload of the trip; a complete suffusion of sagebrush at its utmost essence. It was an experience somewhere between a nirvanic permeation and a sensation as of slowly realizing that you had just eaten far too much blue cheese.

As for the grouse, and the trout this morning, even the cool of the water around the legs—

What you bring home from a hunt or a fishing trip is sometimes not what you went after, most everyone knows that. I have traditional links to the school that claims bagging game doesn't ultimately matter, compared to the blue of the sky and the sun on the sumac up the hill. But today—barred, cut off, left with a few moments of conceptual hookless, rodless fishing: That's pretty thin stuff.

In certain quarters the controversy quietly rages.

~

So I cut across the St. Xavier road and on west over and 'round the Crows' formidable prairie hills to the little village of Pryor, and south from there, then easterly, up into the Pryor Mountains.

The Pryors have been another long-considered destination. I've watched them many times from Interstate 90 up between Hardin and Billings, wondered about their blue-gray sprawl on the horizon, their discrete niche just off the northwest corner of the Bighorn range. But that day I would have a look. I drove slowly up the gravel road through a rock-shouldered valley of inspired geologic flair, pungent with many caves, and pulled off after twenty minutes to eat my lunch. There was a good place below a pine not far from the road. I hadn't seen a soul all the way from Pryor town. Across the valley loomed a flat-topped mountain bare of trees, with a faint sage-colored haze to it. Many of the mountains within sight had a deep red coloration, as did some of the upper Little Bighorn hills. It lends them a rough and raku look. Even the small dirt road snaking downvalley far below was a dark crimson. The afternoon was hot, but the can of beans from under the car seat was bracingly cool.

Slowly, the birdsong of the place began to register, or rather resume at the delicate point when my presence was accepted and absorbed—Lark sparrows, kinglets, juncoes—as the place *filled up* again. I closed my eyes and set myself, configured myself amid the acoustics for a while. Auditory placement as a contemplative mode can make the visual seem shallow, some days: Hearing the horizon gradually widen, the place gradually deepen as the various detail placements are revealed, acknowledged without the overworked eye. (I sometimes think I'll go back east one May for my annual warbler immersion and do nothing but sit in the woodlands under a proper beech with my eyes closed, give one season up to the pure auditory.) Siskins in the ponderosas; those contentious jays far up the hillside. And veeries! Singing in mirror image along the stream down below, no doubt lurking in the dark tunnel of alders on its banks.

And when the eyes opened ten minutes later, there were the larkspurs and the lupines and the familiar peace of the near-at-hand.

But I decided to move to another location, go back toward the Pryor road to a lower spot on the edge of a sage flat where I felt more at home for some odd reason: a plains-plateau place among wild roses, with a desultory Warbling vireo song. Through binoculars I watched a group of Crow cowhands across the valley, talking and smoking in the shade of a horse trailer while their mounts nosed and nibbled in the sagebrush. And there was a cut of long, long vista off to the northwest, toward inner Montana.

If a key component of the contemplative mode—that openness to visitation, that calm attention—is slowness of movement, steadiness of looking, or listening, then that road south from Pryor is a template approach. I doubt I've ever seen a more cratered, washed-out goatpath. If that won't slow you down and get you ready, nothing might.

I was looking at a patch of the remarkable flower I call Crazy Jane (I don't know its actual name, but its post-blossom form resembles a wild head of reckless white hair), thinking that there are two sorts of contemplation/meditation: one that seeks to "escape" the world, float free high above, and one that seeks to engage the world, its details, and follow them to their transcendent implicative plane—the *Full Attention* serving as an "organ" as crucial as a foot or lung.

~

For fifteen years I've been exploring the northern plains. New places, new roads, get scarcer by the month. But that day I whiled a few hours in two new territories.

For fifteen years I've been jumping in the car at any season and taking off, most often alone, driving for three or four days, or ten, two or three hundred easy lesser-road miles per day, looking and looping and sniffing, on full alert all day long until the light wanes. To return home after a week of it with the fine-tuned topography humming inside like a complex musical chord.

And now, of late, I feel an intimacy with the entire area, a familiarity of the type one might attach to a neighborhood in a city or a twenty-acre woodland. There are very few darksides, anymore, to any of the landmark hills or buttes or planos that have gradually become more pertinent than villages and towns. The Highwood Mountains, Bear Butte, the Sweetgrass Hills, Crow and Eaglenest buttes, their various aspects—they hang in a long-layering and humbling intimacy that is, in a word, sedimentary, a function of what Monsieur

Fernand Braudel calls "geographical time." Hot August days with all the windows down.

To glimpse the subtle relations within an immense space, to absorb and house them, in the end becomes as personal and essentially sustaining as one's private memory. To live on a meaningful earth. To come home happy after a week of it, with the afterimage of the space and grassland-spread of it inside, the *perfection* of it realized like a deep chord—that's why I drive in long misshapen circles so much of my time.

WORKS CONSULTED

Martha Beckwith, *Mandan-Hidatsa Myths and Ceremonies.* American Folklore Society, 1938.

Arthur Bent, *Life Histories of North American Jays, Crows, and Titmice.* Smithsonian Institution, 1946.

Alfred Bowers, *Hidatsa Social and Ceremonial Organization.* Smithsonian Institution, 1963.

George Dorsey, *The Pawnee Mythology.* University of Nebraska, 1997.

George Bird Grinnell, *The Cheyenne Indians.* Yale University, 1923.

Joseph Jablow, *The Cheyenne in Plains Indian Trade Relations, 1795–1840.* J. J. Augustin, 1951.

Mark Meloy, *Islands on the Prairie: The Mountain Ranges of Eastern Montana.* Montana Magazine, 1986.

Ezra Pound, *A Walking Tour Through Southern France.* Edited by Richard Sieburth. New Directions, 1992.

Clark Wissler and D. C. Duvall, *Mythology of the Blackfoot Indians.* University of Nebraska, 1995.

MERRILL GILFILLAN is the author of *Magpie Rising: Sketches from the Great Plains,* which won the PEN/Martha Albrand Award for nonfiction; *Sworn Before Cranes,* a collection of short stories that won the Ohio Book Award and was a finalist for the Colorado Book Award; and, most recently, *Burnt House to Paw Paw: Appalachian Notes,* and *Satin Street* (poems), along with some half-dozen other books of poetry. He lives in Boulder, Colorado.

This book's text was designed by Scott L. Perrizo, with composition by Crossings Press of Lyons, Colorado. It was printed and bound by Johnson Printing, Boulder, Colorado.

The text type is Stempel Garamond, issued by the Stempel foundry in 1924, and now available in the digital library of Linotype. It is the only modern Garamond type family to have both the roman and italic based on the original fonts cut by Claude Garamond in the mid-sixteenth century.

The font used for chapter titles is a modern rotunda blackletter, Goudy Thirty, designed in 1942 by Frederick Goudy. It was one of his last fonts and was intended as a tribute to himself—"30" being the journalists' code for "end of story." Original foundry type and digital forms issued by Lanston Type Company.